uncommon
be extraordinary.

jim burns

general editor

uncommon dramas, skits & sketches

CD-ROM INCLUDED

leader's
resource

Published by Gospel Light
Ventura, California, U.S.A.
www.gospellight.com
Printed in the U.S.A.

Previously Published in the Fresh Ideas series as *Skits and Dramas*
(written and compiled by Christian Stanfield and Joel Lusz) in 1998 and
Skit'omatic (compiled by Judith L. Roth) in 1993.

Library of Congress Cataloging-in-Publication Data
Uncommon dramas, skits, and sketches / Jim Burns, general editor.
p. cm.
Includes index.
ISBN 978-0-8307-4791-7 (trade paper)
1. Drama in Christian education. 2. Church group work with youth.
3. Christian youth—Religious life—Drama. I. Burns, Jim, 1953-
BV1534.4.U63 2009
268'.433—dc22
2009036692

All definitions are from the Merriam-Webster online dictionary.
http://www.merriam-webster.com.

Rights for publishing this book outside the U.S.A. or in non-English languages are administered by
Gospel Light Worldwide, an international not-for-profit ministry. For additional information,
please visit www.glww.org, email info@glww.org, or write to Gospel Light Worldwide,
1957 Eastman Avenue, Ventura, CA 93003, U.S.A.

contents

dramas

skits & sketches

walk-ons

introduction

I love great drama. It often communicates a point much more effectively than the spoken word. There are times as a Christian speaker that a drama or sketch has been presented just before I went on to speak and I almost didn't need to give my message because the drama spoke volumes to our hearts.

Christine Stanfield is a great writer of dramas and an excellent actor. She wrote many of the sketches in the drama section, and I am honored that she would allow the youth worker community to use her material. You'll see right away that her material causes students to think. Often her material is funny, but just as often it has a bite to it. Most importantly, her dramas get kids to think about eternal messages.

My friend and fellow youth worker, Joel Lusz, compiled the wild and crazy skit section. Joel did an incredible job of bringing some of the finest loony skits together in this volume. At HomeWord and the HomeWord Center for Youth and Family at Azusa Pacific University, youth workers kept asking us where to find just plain ol' fun-and-nonsense skits for youth groups, retreats and camps and for the lighter moments of youth ministry. Joel has been in youth work for many years and this is his collection of personal favorites. After reading through this section, they have rapidly become my favorites as well.

One of the great highlights of youth work in this generation is more student hands-on involvement. With this volume of dramas and skits, you have the opportunity to get your students who like drama more involved in hands-on ministry. Thanks for your influence in the lives of students and their families.

Jim Burns, Ph.D.
San Juan Capistrano, California

adapt

Read the material, and then ask yourself, *How can I use this with my group? What should I add? What should I take away? How can it be adapted for our group?* In other words, change it to fit your students. Change the language. Update the material. Use the right props and costumes. Adjust. Alter. Tailor-make. Custom-fit. Modify. Adapt!

use props and costumes

Budget some money for buying costuming paraphernalia: dresses, hats, boots, jackets, purses, wigs, oversized clothes, telephones, musical instruments, drums, eyeglasses, sports equipment, and so forth. Ask church members to donate discards or leftovers from garage sales. Ninety percent of the success of a skit rests with the costuming and props. One year, I took $200 out of our youth ministry budget and went thrift shopping. My first stop was the thrift store. After that, I hit garage sales, 99 cent stores, any place with cheap stuff. You'd be amazed at how many good skit props you can buy at places like that with little money. If you're going to do a cowboy skit, get cowboy hats, boots, holsters, vests and whatever else. Make it more real, yet outrageous. Something about putting on costumes helps students loosen up and get into the spirit of the fun.

swallow your pride

If you can't be a fool for Christ, then whose fool are you? Go ahead and put on the makeup, get hit in the face with a pie, put mustard under your arms. Who cares?! This is how walls are broken down and relationships are built. Set an example of fun for your students. Go for it!

keep a record

Have you ever wondered if you have already done a skit or played a game or given a message to the group you're meeting with today? Us too. We have tried to make record keeping as simple and convenient as possible. Next to each activity, message or skit you use, write the date and with which group it was used. You can also jot down notes for new ideas or suggestions for adaptations or improvements.

DRAMAS

drama \ drä-ma \ **1a:** a composition in verse or prose intended to portray life or character or to tell a story usually involving conflicts and emotions through action and dialogue and typically designed for theatrical performance **b:** a movie or television production with characteristics (as conflict) of a serious play **2:** a state, situation or series of events involving interesting or intense conflict of forces.

dramas

Drama can be used to present a serious message or simply to entertain. It can help bring a lesson to life. In our media-oriented society, we need not be shy about using drama to enhance a message.

Drama can be a great icebreaker. A short skit can be performed before, during or after a sermon or lesson. It can be used at seminars, camps, Sunday School, and as a ministry outreach—in missions, soup kitchens, nursing homes and hospitals.

Dramas can bring a sense of reality to a lesson, appealing to several of the senses and to both the visual and audio learners. Youth workers, preachers, teachers and speakers can make references to something the group has experienced in common through a dramatization—a slice of life.

If you have the luxury of having a director, seasoned actors and a stage, you are indeed fortunate. If not, here are some guidelines:

1. Have your actors memorize their scripts whenever possible. If time does not allow, have the actors at least be as familiar as possible with the script. In this case, for the performance have the scripts in less obvious places—in a newspaper, a book, a magazine, on a desk or table. The actors should look down, "pick up" a line, and "say" it to the other actor, rather than reading it off the page.

2. Have appropriate props—even if they're minimal—such as a chair, a table, a briefcase, a skateboard, and so on.

3. Rehearsal is important—even if it's only a readers' theater performance. Give the "actors" at least a couple of minutes to read through the script before "acting" it out.

These three elements will add a sense of reality to the sketch as well as indicate respect for the audience.

eternity placement

topics

Seeking God; salvation; making eternal choices

key verses

Matthew 6:33; 7:7; Luke 11:9; 12:31

cast

Meg, an Eternity Placement counselor
Ted, a seeker
A passerby, disheveled and beaten up

props

A table, two chairs (one on each side of the table), some books (sitting on the table)

scene

The Eternity Placement office.

Meg:	Hello. I'm Meg, your Eternity Placement counselor. *(Extends hand to Ted.)*
Ted:	*(Shakes hands with her.)* Nice to meet you. I'm Ted.
Meg:	So, you're looking for a religion? *(Both sit down.)*
Ted:	Yeah, I feel like there's something missing in my life.
Meg:	*(Trying not to be too obvious, she is reading from the job training manual.)* I know what you mean. I just started working here recently. I haven't made a decision yet on which religion I'll go with; I'm still looking. But I know you've come to the right place. We won't try to influence your decision—we'll just inform you of your options. Tell me a little about yourself first so I can get a feel for the direction you seem to be headed.
Ted:	I'm successful in school and my personal life is okay, but I still feel like there's something missing. I know

dramas

lots of people, but they're all into different things, and very few of them are really content. I'm not sure which way to go.

Meg:	Do you have any religious background at all?
Ted:	When I was younger, my parents were into this real strict religious deal. Everything was considered bad. I looked at their "Don't" list and it was my "Goals-in-Life" list. So I rebelled big time. I wasn't about to do the every-Sunday thing. It wasn't long before my parents quit going to church, too. But now I really feel like there's an empty spot inside that needs to be filled.
Meg:	I can relate to that. *(Looking through a "Religions of the World" manual, trying to appear as normal as possible.)* Now would you be interested in a multiple-god deal or a one-God program?
Ted:	I think I'll stick with one. More than one sounds too complicated.
Meg:	Okay, that eliminates a number of them right off the bat. Do you want a position of involvement in the religion?
Ted:	Like what?
Meg:	We have a guru in Oregon who runs a religious nudist colony. He's lacking a few nude waiters and buspeople for his *au naturel* restaurant.
Ted:	Uh . . . I'm definitely not interested in *that* kind of involvement.
Meg:	Does the colony concept interest you at all?
Ted:	No.
Meg:	Well, how do you feel about religious rituals and the wearing or not wearing of clothes particular to a certain group?
Ted:	Not interested. I would like to keep this as normal as possible.
Meg:	Well, we are certainly narrowing the field now. How about one of the many new-age groups? Lots of variety here. We have the god-is-everything plan, the self-contained and always popular you-are-god plan, and the god-can-be-whoever-or-whatever-you-want-him-or-her-to-be plan.
Ted:	No, thanks.

Meg:	Well now, it does offer reincarnation possibilities. You could return as anything from a penguin to a hibiscus. But, it doesn't appear that the choice is yours.
Ted:	That sounds totally lame. *(Person walks through the room, looking really weird and/or totally thrashed.)*
Ted:	What happened to him [or her]?
Meg:	He [or she] got into a cult that didn't work out for him [or her]. He's [or she's] back looking at some other options.
Ted:	Do you have anything on plain old Christianity?
Meg:	It doesn't look very exciting.
Ted:	That's okay. I'm not looking for excitement. I'm looking for peace.
Meg:	It says here that one of the faith's major tenants is grace.
Ted:	Grace, huh?
Meg:	My guess is she's a large lady who rents office space at their headquarters. She must be an excellent tenant for them to mention her in their description.
Ted:	I think they're talking about a different kind of tenant [tenet]. A camp counselor tried to explain grace to me once—something about undeserved favor from God. I wasn't ready to hear it then. It sounded too simple and too good to be true. I think I'm ready to hear about it now. I'm at least going to check it out. Thanks for your time.
Meg:	No problem. Say, if you find out how we can get inner peace, let me know, will you?
Ted:	Sure will. Bye.
Meg:	Goodbye, and have a nice day!

in the beginning

topic

Creation vs. evolution

key verses

Genesis 1–2

cast

Faith, an evolutionist

Hope, a creationist

Moderator

props

Two chairs and a podium

scene

A debate between theories of creation and evolution.

Moderator:	*(Speaking to audience.)* Welcome to "The Big Bang Debate." Today on our panel, we have Hope, a student of the Bible, representing the creationist point of view; and Faith, a student of biology, representing the evolutionist viewpoint. *(Turns to speak to panelists.)* As you know, I am here to moderate and will keep my comments to a minimum. Panelists will speak in turn, each beginning the discussion with a simple statement. Hope, we'll start with you.
Hope:	In the beginning God created the heavens and the earth.
Faith:	In the beginning there was some stuff. We're not totally sure what, but most likely some gases and particles and atmosphere.
Hope:	The earth was without form and void and there was darkness.

Faith:	The earth resulted from a big bang; some gases and particles exploded and formed earth.
Hope:	God said, "Let there be light," and there was light.
Faith:	The sun was formed in basically the same manner as the earth; it was a very hot planet because of all its gases. It produced light for the earth.
Hope:	God divided the darkness from the light, calling the dark, night and the light, day.
Faith:	Through random chance, after the earth exploded into being, it fell and came to rest on the perfect axis, rotating in such a way for there to be night and day.
Moderator:	I understand if the earth rotated even two degrees off either way, life as we know it would not be able to exist. That's pretty amazing, isn't it? *(Both Hope and Faith agree.)* Continue, please.
Hope:	God separated the heavens from dry land, which He called earth, and the waters, which He called seas.
Faith:	The separation of matter from the skies and then water coming upon the earth all happened from a random sequence of events and perfect atmospheric conditions.
Hope:	God said, "Let the earth bring forth grass and herbs and fruit," and it was so.
Faith:	From primordial ooze, a single-cell organism came into being. This, of course, took billions of years. That single cell eventually evolved into a plant.
Hope:	God created creatures—animals, birds and sea life. He created them male and female.
Faith:	Over billions of years, a single-cell amoeba mutated and eventually an animal evolved. More mutations and males and females eventually developed.
Hope:	God created man in His own image and then He created woman.
Faith:	Over billions of years through genetic mutation, man and monkey evolved from a common ancestor.
Moderator:	Thank you, Hope and Faith. In closing, I'd like to ask each of you, based on your views, what can you look forward to as far as your future is concerned? This time we'll start with Faith.
Faith:	Live life to the fullest, because that's all there is.

dramas

17

| Hope: | To live a fruitful life on earth and then to live forever in heaven with God. |
| Moderator: | Well, you've certainly given us some things to think about. Thanks again. |

dramas

perfect for the job

topic

We are saved by God's grace

key verses

John 3:16-17; Romans 3:22-24; Ephesians 2:8-9; 1 Timothy 1:12-16

cast

Courtney, a job applicant

Grace, the interviewer for the job

props

Two chairs, papers, a clipboard, a portable file, a chalkboard (optional)

scene

A corporate office. Onstage are two chairs and a chalkboard that reads, "INTERVIEWS HERE." Grace is shuffling through papers with a clipboard on her lap. Courtney comes in, dressed nicely and carrying a file.

Courtney:	*(Calling off.)* Through here? Oh, I see. Thanks. *(She crosses to Grace.)* I'm here for the job. *(Fishes out a paper.)* Here's my résumé. Laser-jet printed. Macintosh. *(Taps the paper.)* Linen-finish paper.
Grace:	*(Smiling.)* Very impressive. *(Courtney grins, just standing there.)* You can just have a seat over there. I'll call you.
Courtney:	*(A little disappointed.)* Oh. Fine. *(She sits, notices the audience and leans in.)* I'm not, like, trying to sound uppity or anything, but I'm a shoo-in. I'm perfect for this job. Really. I've worked hard to build up a résumé like that. Took the right courses. Aced 'em all. Extra-curricular stuff. I deserve this position. It's *true*.
Grace:	Courtney?
Courtney:	*(To the audience as she goes to Grace.)* Great résumé, too. Laser-jet printed. Macintosh. Linen-finish paper.

dramas

Grace:	Hello, Courtney. I'm Grace. *(Shakes her hand.)* Please sit down. *(Courtney sits. Grace looks at the résumé.)* Well, Courtney, I have to tell you, this is really an incredible résumé. *(Courtney smiles at the audience.)* I don't think I've seen one better. 3.9 G.P.A. Ninety-eighth percentile on S.A.T. scores. Captain of the debating team. Lettered in track, swimming and golf. French, Spanish, Russian and Mandarin Chinese. Church youth group leader. Honor roll all four years. Type 80 words per minute. Scholarship awards. Your parents must be very proud of you.
Courtney:	Thank you. Yes, they are. I've made sure of it.
Grace:	I'm certain you have. Do you mind if I ask a few questions? *(Courtney shakes her head yes.)* Fine. *(Pulls up clipboard.)* Can you work full-time? Forty to forty-five hours a week?
Courtney:	Yes, I can.
Grace:	Uh-huh. *(Makes a check on the application.)* Nights and weekends okay? *(Courtney nods; Grace checks.)* Do you have your own car?
Courtney:	Yes, I do.
Grace:	*(Checks.)* Have you ever lied to your mother?
Courtney	*(Pauses.)* What?
Grace:	Have you ever lied to your mother?
Courtney:	*(Totally lost.)* Well, I . . . might . . . I think I was out kind of late once . . . and I . . .
Grace:	True or false, Courtney?
Courtney:	True. I mean . . . yes. I have.
Grace:	Uh-huh. *(Checks.)* Have you ever cheated on a test?
Courtney:	No way! I have never, ever!
Grace:	Never?
Courtney:	*(Pause.)* Well, once when I was in the fourth grade.
Grace:	Uh-huh. *(Checks.)*
Courtney:	Wait a minute! I was only nine years old!
Grace:	Have you ever spit on your geeky little brother's tuna sandwich before giving it to him?
Courtney:	Hold on! How'd you know I—?
Grace:	Uh-huh. *(Checks.)*
Courtney:	Time out! What does that prove?
Grace:	I'm afraid you're not perfect.

Courtney:	But I am perfect for the job!
Grace:	Well, according to these answers—
Courtney:	*(Standing.)* Well, then nobody's perfect! If I'm not, *nobody is!* Look, I spit on Frankie's sandwich because he flushed my Care Bear down the toilet. You can't crash me for that! This is insane! I've worked until I could drop! That's great stuff you've got in front of you! I'm the *creme de la creme*! Everybody says so! *(Starts to cry.)* I worked so hard . . . Okay . . . fine . . . I'll . . . I'll just—
Grace:	Relax. You've got the job, Courtney.
Courtney:	How am I going to tell my mom—*(Stops)*. I got the job?
Grace:	You've got the job. I never said you didn't get it.
Courtney:	*(Stunned.)* But—I thought you said—*(Pause)*. Well then, what did I do to deserve the job?
Grace:	Nothing. You didn't do anything.
Courtney:	Oh. *(She sits.)* That's a switch.
Grace:	*(Holding up résumé.)* This doesn't count, understand? Nothing you ever did counts here. You're in here on my word. *(Grace tears up resume and application.)* This is history. Still want the job?
Courtney:	Let me get this straight. Am I going to have to be perfect from now on out?
Grace:	You can try. You won't be. You've got the job either way.
Courtney:	*(Pauses.)* When would you want me to start?
Grace:	Immediately.
Courtney:	*(Thinks, then smiles.)* I'm in.

They shake hands and then exit.

dramas

best friends

topic

Submitting to Jesus

key verses

John 14:15,23-24; Romans 8:7-9; Philippians 2:9-11; James 4:7

cast

Marci, a Christian teenager

Jessica, Marci's non-Christian friend

props

two purses, assorted shopping bags

scene

Marci and Jessica come out of a store, holding shopping bags.

Jessica: *(Checking for her purse.)* Oh, no! I left my purse in there! *(She sees something across the way and squeals quietly.)* There he is! I can't believe it! He's here!

Marci: *(Looking around.)* Who?

Jessica: *(Pointing in a concealed way.)* Danny. Marci, don't let him out of your sight! I'll be right back.

Jessica exits quickly. Marci starts moving toward where Jessica pointed out Danny. She bumps into an invisible Someone.

Marci: *(Tensely.)* Aaah! *(She shushes herself and looks to see who surprised her.)* Oh, it's You. Don't *do* that, Jesus. You scared me to death. What are You doing here, any-way? I mean, this isn't Your usual hangout, is it? *(Marci listens for a moment and looks kind of ashamed.)* Yeah, I know we were supposed to spend some time together, and we will. Really. Just as soon as I get

dramas

home. But I'm with Jessica right now. You want me to witness to my friends, don't You? So that means I've got to spend time with her. Jessica *is* my best friend, You know. *(Marci listens again and gets a determined look on her face.)* No, Jesus, that just wouldn't work. You don't really want to come this time, anyway. You'd be bored, trust me. You'd be better off going back home. *(She looks around.)* Oh, hush. Here comes Jess.

Jessica: *(Tearing out of the store, waving her purse.)* I got it! Is he still there?

Marci: *(Uneasily, blocking the spot where Jesus is standing.)* Who?

Jessica: Danny. Oh, there he is. Hey, he's going into that movie. Come on, Marci! This is the chance I've been waiting for.

Marci: *(Looking uncomfortably at Jesus.)* Uh, wait a minute. I'm not sure I want to see that movie. I heard it has some scenes that aren't very good, if you know what I mean. Besides, I used up all my money.

Jessica: Hey, no problem. I'll pay. Anything to get near to Danny. Just close your eyes during the parts that bother you. Come on, Marci. You know I'd go with you if it were a guy that you liked.

Marci: Oh, all right. *(She glances toward Jesus and then back to Jessica.)* You go ahead and get in line to buy the tickets. I'll be right there.

Jessica: Hurry, okay?

Marci: I will, I will.

Jessica exits.

Marci: *(To Jesus.)* Okay, listen. I'm going with Jessica. I'll be back before You miss me, and I promise I'll close my eyes during the bad parts, okay? *(She listens and begins shaking her head.)* No, You can't come in with us. You don't understand. This really is not Your kind of movie. *(She listens again, feigning patience.)* Yes, I know You wanted to meet Jessica, but I don't think this is the right time. I'll introduce the two of you later, okay? *(She listens again, no longer even trying to be patient.)* I don't know when! Sometime, okay? For now, I just

want to go with her and show her that I'm her friend. Now, You stay here and I'll be back later.

Marci heads toward the movie. Near the place where she would exit, she turns around abruptly.

Marci: Why are You following me? Don't You understand? I don't want You to come with me!

5

the best deal in the world

topic

Eternal life in Christ

key verses

John 6:25-58; Romans 6:23; 1 John 5:11-12

cast

Salesman

Young Man

props

Loud jacket and clashing pants, a Bible, a contract, a pen, signs with slogans as labeled below and a huge toy pencil (optional)

scene

Salesman, dressed in a very loud jacket with clashing pants, is pacing around the floor of a large showroom. Signs cover the room with slogans like, "Why More People Choose the World," "Easy Credit Terms," "What Makes the World So Affordable?" The salesman is obviously only interested in making a sale. A young man carrying a Bible enters the showroom and wanders around aimlessly.

Salesman:	Can I help you?
Young Man:	No . . . I'm just looking.
Salesman:	*(Mocking.)* I'm glad that you told me that. I'll help you find it.
Young Man:	Find what?
Salesman:	Why, whatever you're looking for, of course.
Young Man:	*(Confused.)* What am I looking for? Oh yeah . . . I'm looking for eternal life.
Salesman:	You mean the good life.

dramas

25

Young Man:	No, eternal life. I was just next door, and the guy over there had this great deal. I can get guaranteed eternal life if I just turn my life over to Christ. *(He opens the Bible and points inside.)* The brochure says there's no down payment or anything, but I thought before I make a big decision like that I'd better shop around. What kind of deal can you give me?
Salesman:	Well, you are in the right place, my friend. I'm glad you decided to shop around. I've got the best deal in the world.
Young Man:	On eternal life? That's great!
Salesman:	*(Leaning against object in an attempt to be cool.)* What color did you want? Basic black, passionate purple, neon orange, or my personal favorite, hot-as-hell red?
Young Man:	Wow! Color choices! All I could get at that other place was white.
Salesman:	I didn't even tell you how many shades of gray we have. That's another big favorite.
Young Man:	So, what is all this going to cost me?
Salesman:	*(Aside to audience.)* I love this part. *(With great showmanship to young man.)* Why that's the greatest thing about the world, my friend. It's absolutely free!
Young Man:	Impossible. There's no such thing as a free lunch. It has to cost me something.
Salesman:	Nope. Nothing.
Young Man:	You're lying.
Salesman:	Would I lie to you? *(Short pause.)* Don't answer that, just step in here and let the contract speak for itself. *(They move back to the office.)* Have a seat.
Young Man:	Thanks. *(He starts patting his pockets.)* Now, where did I put those glasses?
Salesman:	Glasses?! You don't need to read it. *(He holds out the contract.)* My friend, just put your signature down there at the bottom. *(Offers a huge toy pencil.)* That's enough for us. We *know* where you live.
Young Man:	*(Feeling pushed.)* Well, at least let me look it over!
Salesman:	Ah . . . it's just your standard run-of-the-mill contract. We can work out the details later. Just sign it. There's a line forming outside. The world's pretty popular these days.

26

Young Man:	*(Reading quickly through the contract.)* Wait a minute! What's this clause about reaping and sowing? You mean I may actually have to suffer the consequences of my actions?
Salesman:	Oh, just ignore that part. How often does that happen, anyway? Skip down to paragraph three. Read about the fun times with all the money and friends you get. The world has a lot to offer, you know.
Young Man:	Yeah, but for how long? It says here that the wages of sin is death.
Salesman:	Well . . . as you travel the road of life there are bound to be a few little bumps here and there.
Young Man:	*(Beginning to see through the salesman's talk.)* Hey, when we are talking about eternal life, I think death is a *big* problem.
Salesman:	*(Getting rattled.)* Boy, you *are* picky, aren't you?
Young Man:	I have a right to be picky. It's my life we're talking about. And look at this eternal damnation clause. I'd be nuts if I signed this.
Salesman:	Look. Obviously, you and I got started off on the wrong foot. *(Leaning forward secretively.)* Listen. You seem like a pretty sharp guy, and I wouldn't do this for just anybody, but . . . I guess I can make an exception in your case. If you sign today, I'll throw in the reincarnation package for nothing. That way if it doesn't work out the first time, you can always come back as an ostrich. Or maybe a cow.
Young Man:	A cow?!
Salesman:	Hey, don't knock it. In some places, that's quite an honor.
Young Man:	I want to do this right the first time. As *me.*
Salesman:	*(Losing patience.)* Who's fooling who, buddy? Everybody is eventually going to die.
Young Man:	I know that. I'm just concerned about where I'll end up. *(Stands up to leave.)* Thank you for your time.
Salesman:	Wait, wait! You're passing up the deal of a lifetime. The world could be gone tomorrow.
Young Man:	*(Pauses.)* I know. That's what I'm worried about.

The young man exits.

Salesman: Man, that's the second one I've lost today. I should have told him about the rebate. *(Suddenly brightens up as he looks offstage. Talks while exiting.)* Oh, hi! Come on in! I've got the best deal in the world!

6

the in-crowd

topic
Conforming to Christ, not the world

key verses
Romans 12:12; Galatians 1:10; 1 Peter 1:14-16

cast
Jan, a teenager
Carol, Jan's friend
Girl, a student
The In-crowd, six to eight teenagers

props
T-shirts, jeans, suspenders, sneakers, neckties, sunglasses and headbands
for eight to ten girls; textbooks; a bench

scene
The In-crowd is dressed alike in T-shirts, jeans, suspenders and sneakers
with the other props in their pockets. The In-crowd moves together in
close formation at all times, walking tightly bunched together in a quick-
stepping manner from place to place. They separate just enough to perform each action, returning afterward to close formation, holding their
pose until their next move. One person is designated leader for the rest to
follow. Jan and Carol are typical students, dressed appropriately, but not
in jeans. Carrying textbooks, they enter talking and sit on a bench at
stage left.

Jan:	I can't believe that Mr. Richards! He gave us enough homework to sink the Titanic. And it's due tomorrow. I'll be lucky if I finish half of it by tomorrow.
Carol:	I know what you mean. But I don't see why you're worrying. You get *As* in everything. Of course, you do spend hours studying.

Jan:	Yeah, that's about all I ever do. I like getting good grades, but there ought to be *something* else in life. I really thought high school was going to be a lot more fun than this!
Carol:	Me, too. Nothing but classes and homework. What a drag!
Jan:	*(Sighing.)* Life is pretty dull, all right. *(Chanting)* We go to school, we go home, we do homework, we go to church, we go back to school, we go home, we go to church . . . Bor-r-ring!
Carol:	Oh look, Jan! Look! Here comes the In-crowd!

In-crowd enters from stage left, crosses diagonally behind the girls to the opposite side of the stage. They fold their arms and stand with their bodies slanted toward one hip.

Jan:	Wow! They are *so* awesome!
Carol:	And popular! Wouldn't you just die to be popular like that?
Jan:	Are you kidding? Who wouldn't? Look! Where are they going now?

In-crowd moves to the back of the stage and rolls up the legs of their jeans.

Carol:	Maybe we ought to make ourselves more conspicuous so they will know we're here.
Jan:	Can't hurt to try.

Jan and Carol leave their books on the bench and edge a few feet toward center stage. In-crowd moves center stage and puts some neckties over their T-shirts.

Carol:	Oh, wow! How did they ever think of *that*?
Jan:	Because they're with it, that's how. That's what it takes to be in the In-crowd.

In-crowd moves to position behind an empty bench and puts on sunglasses. Jan and Carol move to center stage.

Jan:	I think they looked at us.

| Carol: | Really? I can't believe it! |
| Jan: | Really! Quick, put on your sunglasses and stand this way. |

Jan and Carol put on sunglasses and stand with their arms folded, leaning on one hip. They try to appear nonchalant. The In-crowd waves to them.

| Jan: | Carol! They're waving at us! What do you think it means? |
| Carol: | They like us, that's what! Oh, wow, I think they're coming over! |

In-crowd approaches and all exchange high-five hand slaps with the girls. The In-crowd moves to stage right, absorbing Jan and Carol into the group. All put on headbands.

Jan:	Isn't this great? I've never had so much fun!
Carol:	Me neither. Wonder what they will think of next?
Jan:	I don't know, but whatever it is, it'll be a blast!

In-crowd moves to stage left, roughing up their hair, dropping their suspenders to hang over their hips.

Carol:	I wonder when they do their homework? All this running around takes up a lot of time. Not that it isn't fun, of course.
Jan:	We probably won't have much time for homework from now on. Not if we want to keep up with these guys. You have to be dedicated.
Carol:	Yeah, I can see that. Hurry! We're going again!

Girl walks across from stage right, reading a book. In-crowd moves to center stage, crashing into her and knocking her down. In-crowd doesn't stop moving, trampling over the girl to reach a new position, stage right. Jan and Carol stop as the crowd leaves the fallen girl and run back to help her.

Jan:	Are you all right?
Carol:	Here's your book. It's not hurt, just a little dirty.
Girl:	Oh, thank you. I'm okay, really. I just didn't see them coming. But I know that bunch. It doesn't pay to get

in their way. They never look where they're going. Were you with them?

Jan and Carol look ashamed and take off their sunglasses and headbands.

Jan: I don't know if you would say that we were really *with* them . . .

Carol: We were sort of hanging around them, but only for a little while.

Girl: Hey, aren't you Jan Taylor? Sure, you're in my brother's history class. Don Riley. Know him?

Jan: Well, I know who he is. You're his sister? How did you know me?

Girl: He pointed you out once. He thinks you're pretty cool. Says you're a brain! I think he likes you.

Jan: Wow! He said that? And he thinks I'm smart?

Girl: Too smart to get mixed up in a crowd like that, that's for sure. Well, I've got to go. Thanks for your help. See you around!

Jan and Carol: Bye!

Girl exits stage left as In-crowd walks backward in a synchronized fashion off stage right. Jan and Carol walk to the bench for their books.

Jan: I guess the In-crowd wasn't all that we thought it would be.

Carol: Yeah. They don't seem to care about much but themselves!

Jan: If that's what it takes to be popular, I'd rather not try.

Carol: Well, you're still popular with me, and maybe with a guy named Don, too! *(Teasing.)* Did I get his name right? Hmm?

Jan: Real funny. Cut it out, Carol.

Carol: *(Laughing.)* Maybe he's got a brother.

Jan: You know what, Carol? You're pretty fun, even if you're not one of the In-crowd. Hey, let's go to Bible study tomorrow night, okay? We haven't been all summer and—

Carol: I know what you mean. I guess if we're going to follow anyone, it ought to be Jesus.

7

eternal fire protection

topics

Forgiving others; turning from sin; accepting salvation

key verses

Mark 11:25; Luke 6:37; Luke 13:3; 2 Corinthians 7:10; 1 John 1:9

cast

Eddy, a tough street punk with a Brooklyn accent
Mrs. Goldstein, a New York housewife with a nasally voice
Fireman Clint, an unemotional, monotone, just-the-facts-ma'am kind of guy
Fireman Rambo, a tough, muscle-laden man of action

props

About five red rocks, two fireman hats, a megaphone (optional)

scene

Eddy runs on stage, juggling four or five bright red rocks, blowing on his hands and shouting, "Ow, woo, hot, hot, hot. OUCH! HOT! HOT! HOT!" Mrs. Goldstein, walking down the street, sees Eddy and lets out a scream.

Mrs. Goldstein: Oh my! This man is burning up! Somebody help!

Off in the distance, the self-made siren sounds of Firemen Clint and Rambo are heard. The two run out, continuing to scream the siren noise, run around the audience, circle the stage and come to a screeching halt in front of Mrs. Goldstein.

Clint: What seems to be the problem here?!
Mrs. Goldstein: *(Pointing frantically at Eddy.)* Are you blind? There's a man holding red-hot rocks, and he's going to burn up! You've got help him!

© 2009 Gospel Light. Permission to photocopy granted. *Uncommon Dramas, Skits and Sketches.*

33

dramas

Clint:	Okay, calm down, ma'am. Now, give me just the facts.
Mrs. Goldstein:	I told you! *(She shakes Clint.)* He's going to burn up, and you've got to help him!
Clint:	We'll do our best, ma'am.
Rambo:	*(Suddenly jumping out in front of the others.)* Stand back! We may have to hose him down!

Mrs. Goldstein backs away and peers over the shoulders of the two firemen, watching the events with concern.

Clint:	*(Picking up a megaphone and shouting to Eddy.)* Don't be afraid, son! We're here to help you! Throw down those burning coals and we'll put them out and give you some first aid!
Eddy:	No!
Clint, Rambo and Mrs. Goldstein:	*(Together.)* No?! What do you mean, no?
Eddy:	I said, No, ooh, ooh, hot, hot.
Clint:	But you're burning up!
Eddy:	Look, everyone's a critic. Do I go around criticizing and bad-mouthing you, huh? Huh? Yo, hot, hot, ooh, oooh!
Rambo:	*(Shouting to Eddy as if he were far away.)* But we're here . . . to help . . . you!
Eddy:	Why don't you mind . . . your own . . . business?!
Clint:	But those things could kill you!
Eddy:	Hey, look. When I go, I go. I don't think about it.
Rambo:	Hey, do you mind if I have a look at those things?
Eddy:	Well . . . okay, I guess so.

Rambo takes off his hat, and Eddy dumps the rocks into it. While Eddy rests from his torment, the three gather around the open hat.

Rambo:	Just as I thought!
Mrs. Goldstein:	What?
Rambo:	This is eternal fire! Even if we hosed it down, tossed it in the ocean, flew it to Alaska and threw it in the snow, this stuff would never go out! *It burns forever!*
Eddy:	Shut up! *(He snatches the rocks back and begins to juggle them again.)* Yo, hot, hot, ohhh, yow, ow!

Clint:	Son, you're in big trouble! Get rid of this stuff now before it takes you with it!
Eddy:	Come on! It's not that serious! It's just a way of life.
Mrs. Goldstein:	I don't know why you're holding on to those things, but what I want to know is, how did you get them in the first place?
Eddy:	Well, I had this burning hatred for this person, and one of these showed up in my hands. Someone did me wrong, and I wouldn't forgive him, and another one of these showed up! Then I had this burning jealously and stole some stuff . . . and all these things kept showing up in my hands.
Clint:	Son, don't you see? It's not going to stop! Even after you die, those things will keep burning you. God can't let you into heaven with those things!
Eddy:	Hey . . . hey . . . Ow! I don't think a God of love would make me burn!
Rambo:	Is God making you burn now?
Eddy:	Uh . . . well, uh . . . No. I'm the one who's holding on.
Rambo:	God doesn't want you to burn!
Clint:	In fact, God sent His Son, Jesus, to put out the eternal fire in people's hearts. He can put out your eternal fire, too, if you ask Him.
Eddy:	Look! I'm a self-made man. This religion stuff burns me up! Look, I've got to go. See you. Ow, oh, hot, hot, yow!

Eddy exits, still juggling the rocks.

Mrs. Goldstein:	That's sad!
Rambo:	It sure is!
Clint:	Let's help someone who *wants* to have his fire put out!

The firemen start the siren and zoom off. Mrs. Goldstein runs after them.

dramas

35

8

can God's love be measured?

topic
God's unconditional and unwavering love

key verses
John 3:16; Romans 8:38-39

cast
Brian
Brian's mom
Angel One, a mature, sensible angel
Angel Two, a goofy, very enthusiastic angel
Angel Three, a stern, slightly grumpy angel

props
A chair and small table or desk, a writing tablet and pen or pencil, a notebook, a chalkboard with chalk and eraser (or make a "Love-O-Meter" poster), a pamphlet resembling a Bible study handout

scene
Brian's room.

Brian: *(Talking to self as he writes.)* Brian Whitney, [say the date skit is being performed]. "How Much Does God Love Me?" *(Stops writing.)* My first year at a Christian school and I have to write a whole page about how much God loves me. I don't know how much He loves me. Sometimes I think He loves me pretty much, but sometimes I don't think He loves me that much. I've got to think about this for a while. *(He takes a deep breath, puts his head down on the table/desk and falls asleep.)*

36

10

Angels One, Two and Three enter and position poster or chalkboard so that audience can see. On the board is a dial graph with the title "God's Love-O-Meter," which reads as follows:

Angel Two:	*(Turns to Angel One and extends hand.)* Greetings! I'm the angel in charge of the "good-stuff-kids-do" department, reporting for work. *(Turns slightly to the audience, winks and whispers.)* It's my first day on the job.
Angel Three:	*(Shaking hand of Angel One firmly.)* Hello, I'm the angel in charge of the not-so-good-stuff-kids-do department, reporting for work. *(Turns slightly to the audience and matter-of-factly announces.)* I'm a veteran of this job.
Angel One:	It's heavenly to be working with both of you. I'm the angel in charge of God's Love-O-Meter. *(Moves the dial in an exaggerated manner.)* We have the following categories, with reference to degrees of love: "Almost None," "A Little Bit," "Medium," "Pretty Much" and "Major Huge." Right now we'll be looking at Brian Whitney for his afternoon scoring. For a quick review, each of you will be giving me a rundown on Brian's behavior. I will adjust the dial on the Love-O-Meter accordingly. What we come up with at the end will be the amount of love he is receiving as of this afternoon. We will, of course, return at his bedtime for the final score of this day. As I'm sure you recall, at

the end of our noon meter scoring, Brian ended with "A Little Bit" of love based on his talking in class when he was supposed to be listening to his teacher.

Angel Two: I'd like to point out that at lunchtime at Brian's school, a girl dropped her tray of food and he helped her pick up the stuff even though his friends were making fun of him. That would put him up to "Major Huge" love, right?

Angel One: (Gently sarcastic.) I don't think so. It will bring his score up to "Pretty Much" love but no higher.

Angel Three: However, as soon as he got home, he started bugging his little brother and caused him to start screaming . . .

Angel One: Tut, tut, tut. (Moves the dial to "A Little Bit.")

Angel Three . . . while his mom was trying to talk on the phone.

Angel One: Oh . . . (Moves the dial to "Almost None.")

Angel Two: But after he got in trouble for that, he took the dishes out of the dishwasher and put them away without being asked, which I would think would bring him up to "Pretty Much" love.

Angel One: (Sarcastic.) Yeah, right. The fact is that will take him to "Medium" love.

Angel Three: However, when his mother read the note from the teacher about the talking-in-class problem and she sat Brian down to talk about it, he talked back to her.

Angel One: Tut, tut, tut! (Moves the dial to "A Little Bit.")

Angel Two: But when he was sent to his room, he started on his homework without being told to. That has to bring him back up to "Pretty Much" love.

Angel One: That's absolutely right—NOT! It is very obvious this is your first day on the job. Actually, it will take him to "Medium" love and that's where he stops for this afternoon.

Angel Two: What about . . .

The three angels continue to discuss while Brian stretches his arms and opens his eyes.

Brian: (Talking to himself.) I wonder if that's what happens? I don't know.

Mom: Brian?

dramas

38

Brian:	Yeah, Mom?
Mom:	I was thinking about that writing assignment you have because we're studying the subject of love in my women's Bible study. I came across these two really good verses that might help you. *(Hands him pamphlet.)* Oh, you're already working on your assignment. That's good, honey. I'll call you when dinner is ready.
Brian:	*(Reads the verses aloud.)* John 3:16: "For God so loved the world that he gave his one and only Son that whoever believes in him shall not perish but have eternal life." Hmm. *(Pauses and thinks for a moment.)* Romans 8:38-39: "For I am convinced that neither death nor life, neither angels nor demons, neither the present nor the future, nor any powers, neither height nor depth, nor anything else in all creation, will be able to separate us from the love of God that is in Christ Jesus our Lord." *(Pauses and reflects on what he has just read.)* Wow, I guess there really isn't a Love-O-Meter for how much God loves me. I'd better check out the Bible to get the truth. *(Calls out as he exits.)* Mom, where's my Bible?

tough love

topics
Loving enough to confront; sacrifice; true friendship

key verses
Ecclesiastes 3:7; Psalm 49:3; Proverbs 8:7

cast
Two friends, guys or girls
Carla (or Carl, if male actor)
Mandy (or Manny, if male actor)

props
Basketball or 4-square ball, wall to bounce ball against

scene
Carla's house as Mandy arrives.

Carla:	*(Bouncing ball against wall; looks at Mandy.)* What are you doing here?
Mandy:	I wanted to talk to you, and since you haven't returned any of my phone calls, I'm here.
Carla:	Well, I don't want to talk to you. That's why I didn't return any of your calls.
Mandy:	Nice way to treat your best friend.
Carla:	My ex-best friend.
Mandy:	Look, Carla, I did what I thought was best for you.
Carla:	Oh, thank you so much. My life has just been wonderful since you told my parents I was using drugs.
Mandy:	I said you were experimenting with drugs.
Carla:	Excuse me—"experimenting"? That makes such a big difference.
Mandy:	Yes, it does. I tried to talk to you, but you wouldn't listen. Do you think it was easy for me to tell your folks?

Carla:	Now I'm supposed to feel sorry for you?
Mandy:	No, I just wanted to tell you that it was a very difficult decision. If I didn't care, I wouldn't have done it.
Carla:	I'd rather you didn't do me any more favors, okay?
Mandy:	You think your life would have been great if you'd continued doing drugs?
Carla:	I had no intention of continuing forever.
Mandy:	Do you think anyone does? I seriously doubt that anybody says, *(mockingly)* "I think I'll be a drug addict. That sounds like a constructive lifestyle."
Carla:	Amusing, Mandy. Ben said he'd tried a few things and it was kind of fun, so he offered me some pills. I only took one every once in a while.
Mandy:	And smoked a few joints now and then.
Carla:	So what? It was no big deal.
Mandy:	Well, I think it was. You started hanging out with a different crowd; your grades went down. You . . .
Carla:	*(Interrupting.)* Thanks, but I've already heard this lecture. Why don't you go preach to someone who wants to hear it!
Mandy:	Okay, I'll leave, but I wanted to tell you that you're still my best friend and I'll stick by you no matter what.
Carla:	Yeah, right. Just get out of here! You've ruined my life.
Mandy:	*(As she exits.)* No, I didn't, but you were about to.

dramas

promises

topic

Putting your faith and trust in God

key verses

Joshua 1:5,9

cast

Four friends:

    Sarah

    Larry

    Julie

    Carl

Paul, the new kid at school

Mom, Paul's mother

props

Five lunch boxes or bags, schoolbooks, a backpack, several papers folded to resemble a Sunday School handout, a bell to ring offstage, a desk or small table, a chair for desk, paper for note

scene one

Sarah, Larry, Julie and Carl sit cross-legged on ground at lunchtime, each looking through their lunches.

Paul:	*(Enters stage and walks toward group.)* Hi, Sarah.
Sarah:	*(Uncomfortable about knowing the new kid.)* Hi.
Paul:	*(Walks past group and sits alone.)*
Larry:	Who's that, Sarah?
Julie:	The new kid.
Carl:	*(Tauntingly.)* Oh, so Sarah gets the new kid for a boyfriend.
Sarah:	*(Quietly.)* He's not my boyfriend.
Larry:	*(Tauntingly.)* He *likes* you.

dramas

Sarah:	You don't know that! He happens to be in my class, so he knows my name—it's no big deal.
Larry:	I bet he hasn't been welcomed to Jefferson School yet.
Sarah:	Yes, he has. I heard him telling our teacher that someone jammed his gym locker shut with towels.
Larry:	*(Points to Carl as if to ask, "You?")*
Carl:	*(Gives a thumbs-up—both boys give high fives.)*
Julie:	*(Giggles.)* You guys are so funny.
Sarah:	*(Disgustedly.)* Oh, yeah, real funny and so mature, too.
Carl:	Well, you're so boring and immature.
Larry:	Forget it. Let's get on to the other part of the welcome. Sarah, since you're his buddy, go talk to him so I can grab his lunch box.
Sarah:	What for? What are you going to do now?
Larry:	Don't worry about it. We're not going to hurt your little Pauly.
Sarah:	He's not my little Pauly, but I still don't want any part of your so-called welcome.
Carl:	You are such a pansy. Okay, Julie, you go distract him. Ready for Plan B, Larry?
Julie:	*(Gets up and walks toward Paul.)*
Larry:	Yep. I'll grab the box, pass it off to you and you know what to do with it.
Julie:	*(To Paul.)* Hi, my name's Julie.
Paul:	I'm Paul.
Julie:	I heard you're new here.
Paul:	Yeah. Are you friends with Sarah?
Larry:	*(Sneaks up and takes Paul's lunch box, and then hands it over to Carl.)*
Carl:	*(Exits with Paul's lunch and comes back without it.)*
Julie:	Yeah, we're friends. Well, I'd better get back and finish my lunch.
Paul:	Okay. Bye. *(He turns around and starts looking for his lunch box.)*
Sarah:	Carl, what did you do with it?
Carl:	*(Ignores Sarah.)* Hey, everyone look up on the roof! What is that? *(Everyone except Sarah looks up.)*
Sarah:	*(Stands up.)* I'm leaving.
Larry:	*(Loudly.)* It looks like a lunch box to me!
Carl:	I wonder whose it is.

dramas

43

| Larry: | I wonder how it got there. |
| Carl: | Maybe aliens from outer space put it there. *(Larry, Carl and Julie giggle.)* |

Bell rings offstage and everyone exits.

scene two

Paul arrives home from school.

Paul:	*(Calls out as he enters stage.)* Mom, I'm home! *(Drops backpack and picks up note from table—reads it aloud.)* "Paul, I had to run over to Grandma's for just a few minutes. I'll be right back. Please straighten up your room. Love, Mom." *(Begins to exit room and notices Sunday School paper on desk—picks it up and reads aloud.)* Joshua 1:5: "As I was with Moses, so I will be with you; I will never leave you nor forsake you." *(Looks through some more papers and reads aloud.)* Joshua 1:9: "Have I not commanded you? Be strong and courageous. Do not be terrified; do not be discouraged, for the LORD your God will be with you wherever you go." *(Sits at desk as if to think about what he just read.)*
Mom:	*(Calls out as she enters stage.)* Paul? I'm home!
Paul:	*(Gets up from desk as mom enters room.)* Hi, Mom.
Mom:	*(Goes to him and gives him a hug.)* Hi, honey. How was your day?
Paul:	Not good. The principal said I'd fit right in, but I'm not. My teacher said the kids would be nice to me, but they aren't. I thought one girl in my class was going to be nice, but she wasn't. Then I thought this one kid in my gym class was trying to be my friend, but he just wanted to play a joke on me.
Mom:	I'm sorry, honey. You know, kids can be mean sometimes, especially when someone is new at school. Do you want me to talk to the principal?
Paul:	No. I don't think it would help. It just seemed like people were breaking their promises all day. I know they weren't really promises, but it seemed like it. It made me sad. Then I was feeling lonely walking home by myself and when I got home you weren't here. But

44

	when I was cleaning my desk, I read some of my Scripture verses from Sunday School and I prayed. I feel lots better now.
Mom:	I'm sorry I wasn't here when you got home. I want you to know I'm so proud of you. That was the best thing you could do. There are so many Scripture promises that can help us. And of course taking our problems to God in prayer is always a good idea.
Paul:	Yeah, I know that even when I'm by myself, I'm not alone. God is always with me.
Mom:	You're exactly right. You know, the Bible is full of God's promises for us. People don't always keep their promises, but God always keeps His. So are you feeling good enough for a snack?
Paul:	Yeah, I'm starving. I didn't eat lunch.
Mom:	Why not?
Paul:	*(As they exit together.)* It's a long story, involving aliens from outer space.
Mom:	Oh.

the s.a.t. of life

topic
Trusting in God

key verses
Psalm 62:8; Proverbs 3:5-6; John 14:1; 2 Corinthians 1:8-11

cast
voice
Chris
Ms. New-Age
Timid Tina
Mr. Checkout
Cheater

props
Five chairs, five pencils, test-like booklets, a cell phone, a crystal, a mirror, a chalkboard (optional)

scene
Five anxious students are sitting in chairs: Timid Tina, Ms. New-Age, Cheater, Mr. Checkout and Chris. A chalkboard behind reads, "The S.A.T. of Life" and "No Talking." The students are all talking.

Voice: *(From offstage.)* Good morning. Welcome, students, to the Great S.A.T. of Life. There will be no talking, eating, chewing gum or drinking during the test. Please fill in each correct bubble on your answer sheet with a Number 2 pencil. Fill in the bubbles completely. Don't take too long on each question. Remember, you have 60 to 70 years to complete the test. You may turn your books over now.

They turn over the books. There is a collective groan.

| All: | I should have studied more! |
| Voice: | *(Offstage.)* Shh! |

They begin to read. Cheater rolls back his pant leg and reads notes written on his ankle. Ms. New-Age looks around the room. Chris, who sits a little bit apart, watches everyone.

Chris:	*(To Ms. New-Age.)* Why aren't you working on the test?
Ms. New-Age:	What test? There is no test. I'm in an out-of-body experience right now. My crystal is warm. There is no test.
Chris:	But it's right in front of you. On the table.
Ms. New-Age:	*(Almost chanting.)* There is no test . . . there is no test. *(Chris holds it up in front of her face.)* Oh, that test. *(Disgruntled, she begins to read.)*

Cheater has slid off his belt and is reading notes written on the backside of it. Timid Tina looks around and then pulls out a cell phone from under her jacket.

| Timid Tina: | *(Whispering.)* Mom, I don't have any answers. Help me, will you? I can't do it alone. |

Mr. Checkout sits with arms folded, looking ahead.

Ms. New-Age:	*(To Mr. Checkout.)* Are you looking for your center?
Mr. Checkout:	Nah, I'm just not taking the stupid test.
Ms. New-Age:	If you can only find your inner self, you'll be able to—
Mr. Checkout:	Get out of here. I'm not taking the test because no one has any of the answers. It's a waste of time. Even if you came up with an answer and filled in the bubble, it's only your opinion.

Ms. New-Age shakes her head, wide-eyed. Cheater lifts up the collar of the person in front of him and looks for notes.

| Timid Tina: | *(Dials.)* Hello, Ms. Landers. This is Tina from your history class. I'm not ready for this test. Can you give me some answers? Could you take the test for me? |

dramas

Ms. New-Age looks at Chris, whose eyes are closed in prayer.

Ms. New-Age:	*(Almost squealing.)* Oh, you're finding your center!
Chris:	No. My place.
Ms. New-Age:	Your place is in the center. The center of everything. You are everything. Want my crystal?
Chris:	I'm not meditating. I'm praying.

Everyone looks at Chris.

Mr. Checkout:	To God? Dude, give it up. You won't get any answers. It's a one-sided conversation.
Ms. New-Age:	Well, that's almost like meditating.
Cheater:	Does God have Cliff's Notes?
Timid Tina:	You got His phone number?
Voice:	*(Offstage.)* Shhhhh!

They go back to work. Ms. New-Age holds a crystal to her forehead. Chris goes back to prayer. Timid Tina starts tapping on her phone.

Timid Tina:	There must be some app here that can give me the answers—

Cheater holds up a mirror in an attempt to see the test in front of him.

Chris:	Lord, I don't know all the answers. I really don't. I read up all I could. I went to all the studies I could. It's just that I don't know the answers to some of these questions. I don't understand them.
Timid Tina:	*(Dials.)* Can you put me through to the Mahareeshi Yogibeary?

Cheater pulls a piece of paper out of his nose (or mouth) and reads it.

Chris:	Lord, You know my heart. I want to do the right thing. None of these people around here are getting anywhere on this test. They don't have any answers. Mr. Checkout over there doesn't even believe there *are* any answers. Cheater can't find any answers for himself. *(Points his thumb at Timid Tina.)* She's calling

everyone in town, hoping someone will give her the answers. Ms. New-Age doesn't even know she's on the planet. *(Sighs.)* Well, I'm just going to start. I'm just going to pick up this pencil and lean on You.

Ms. New-Age: There is no test. No test. I float on clouds of warm liquid. No test . . . no test.

Mr. Checkout: No answers. There are no answers.

Timid Tina: What do you mean the Dalai Lama won't take a collect call?

Cheater takes off his shoe and reads notes on his foot.

Chris: Lord, thank You for my brains, my common sense and Your direction. I commit myself to You. *(He picks up his pencil and starts working.)*

the hitchhiker

topic

God is all-powerful

key verses

Isaiah 40:22-31; Ephesians 1:18-21; 2 Peter 1:3

cast

John, the driver
Sandra, John's girlfriend
Martin, John's friend
Bill, a hitchhiker

props

four chairs, two flashlights, schoolbooks, a shirt and tie, a small Bible

scene

John and Sandra are waiting in John's car in the school parking lot to give Martin a ride. They have flashlights hidden for use later on in the skit.

John:	I hope he didn't get detention or something stupid like that. Does he know we're waiting out here?
Sandra:	Yes, for the third time. Will you please calm down. You're stressing me out. I saw him at break. Quit freaking out, he'll be here. Look, there he is now.
John:	Finally. My blood sugar was getting low.
Martin:	How do, my friends! You are all looking mighty cool today.
Sandra:	Where have you been? We've been waiting for you.
Martin:	*(Undaunted.)* Hey, get this question I heard in science today: Can God make a rock so big He can't lift it?
John:	Of course. After all, He made your brain so small you can't find it! Would you get in the car already? I'm at death's door for lack of greasy food.

Martin hops in the two-door car, crawling over John to get to the back seat. John pulls out into traffic and begins the drive.

Sandra:	McDee's?
John:	Taco Bell. There's a burrito waiting for me.
Martin:	Pizza. A combo represents all four food groups.
John:	I'm driving.
Sandra:	Taco Bell sounds great.
John:	Oh, man, it's stop-and-go traffic. I can't believe it. I hate this parkway.
Martin:	It's too early. There must have been an accident.
Sandra:	Now I'm hungry.
John:	Hey, look at this guy hitching. He must have run out of gas.
Martin:	Nice tie, too. That'll be a goner soon.
John:	Let's give him a ride.
Sandra:	*(Looking at John, shocked.)* I thought you were hungry. Now we have time for this guy?
Martin:	*(Uneasy.)* I don't think that's such a great idea, John. What if he tries to attack us or something?
John:	Give me a break, Martin. What are the chances of that happening? He's wearing a tie. Besides, there's three of us.
Sandra:	Two of you. I'm not helping you beat up anybody.

John pulls over. Bill (the hitchhiker) enters and comes to Sandra's side. John rolls down Sandra's window and leans over to speak.

John:	Where you headed?
Bill:	My car stalled on the other side of the tunnel. Just get me back through the tunnel and I'll be fine.
John:	Sure, hop in, uh . . .
Bill:	Bill. Thanks a million for stopping. I thought I was going to have to hoof it the whole way.

Sandra gets out so Bill can climb in the back seat. Then Sandra climbs back in. John pulls back into traffic.

John:	You might get there faster by walking, Bill. This traffic is brutal.

Bill:	That's okay. At least I'm out of the cold.
Martin:	Uh . . . Bill. I'm Martin. *(They shake hands.)* Nice to meet you. *(Bill nods.)* Would you mind if I asked you a question?
Bill:	Fire away.
Martin:	We've never met, so you can be very honest about your answer. Can God make a rock so big He can't lift—
John:	Martin! He just wants a ride. He doesn't care about—
Bill:	God is all-powerful. He can do anything He wants. He is God.

The car is silent. Bill's response has surprised everyone.

Sandra:	You sound like my dad!
John:	If God were all-powerful, He'd get us out of this traffic jam.
Martin:	God doesn't care about that stuff. Earthquakes, tornadoes, floods. That's His department.
Bill:	Martin, Luke 12:7 says, "The very hairs of your head are numbered." Matthew 6:26 says that God even makes sure that the birds have something to eat. God knows what color socks you put on this morning. He cares about things that small.
Sandra:	Hey, the traffic cleared up.

Everyone turns to look at Bill. He shrugs knowingly.

John:	You don't think He did that, do you?
Bill:	What do you think?
John:	I don't think so. What about you? He let your car run out of gas.
Bill:	You're giving me a ride, aren't you? *(Silence.)* Jesus said in Matthew 17:20 that if you have faith as small as a mustard seed, you can tell a mountain to move and it will.
Martin:	Sounds like you've known God a long time. I can't have that much faith. I need more proof.
Bill:	Here, I have this little Bible. *(He pulls a small Bible from his pocket.)* I'd like you to read this passage right here.

Bill hands the Bible over to Martin. As soon as Martin gets the Bible, there is an immediate blackout. As soon as the darkness is complete, Bill should exit as quickly and as quietly as possible. John and Sandra both pull their hidden flashlights out and turn them on to represent headlights.

Martin:	*(Laughing.)* I'd love to read this passage, Bill, but it's a little dark in here. I think, Bill . . . Bill? You guys, Bill's not in the car anymore!!
John:	Maybe he saw his car and got out.
Martin:	We're going 30 miles an hour and this is a two-door! Did he crawl over either of your backs to get out?!
Sandra:	I don't like this at all, guys. This isn't funny.

Full lights. The actors douse the flashlights.

John:	Holy smokes, you're not kidding. He's gone!
Martin:	Listen to this passage, you guys. Luke 24:31-32: "Then their eyes were opened and they recognized him, and he disappeared from their sight. They asked each other, 'Were not our hearts burning within us while he talked with us on the road and opened the Scriptures to us?' "

There is silence in the car for a moment.

Sandra:	Maybe God *can* do whatever He wants.

53

the opera wimpy show

topic

God helps us change

key verses

Romans 12:2; 1 Corinthians 10:13; 2 Corinthians 3:17-18; Philippians 4:13

cast

Announcer

Opera Wimpy

Jim Hazelnut

Audience member

Cheryl Nada

Susan Gunnersma

Michael Cleanbill

props

microphone, a candy wrapper, index cards, a candy bar, army fatigues, a large box of chocolates, assorted vegetables (optional)

scene

In the studio of a television talk show.

Announcer:	(*Offstage.*) And now, live from Warmwater, Illinois, please welcome TV's most-loved talk-show host—Opera Wimpy!

Opera Wimpy enters carrying a microphone and index cards.

Opera:	(*Into the microphone.*) Welcome to the *Opera Wimpy Show*. "Be not conformed to this world but be transformed by the renewing of your mind." A tall order. God's or-

dramas

der. A big question. Just how do we change our lives? Often we get caught up in behaviors and lifestyles we simply don't want to be part of anymore. Well, today we're going to talk about how to make changes in our lives by tackling the topic of . . . chocolate. Any chocolate lovers in the audience? Well, let's meet some recovering chocoholics to see just how they changed their own lives. Jim Hazelnut, where are you?

Jim: *(Standing; shaky and nervous. He digs through his pockets as he speaks.)* Here, Opera. *(Opera walks over to him, microphone outstretched.)* Hi, my name's Jim, and I'm a recovering chocoholic.

Opera: This chocolate thing—it's a tough nut to crack. How did you do it?

Jim: Well, Opera, I was in big truffle . . . trouble! I sat in my home out in caramel—Carmel! Shoveling in the cho . . . cho . . . cho . . .

Opera: Chocolate.

Jim: Chocolate! I had to have it. Night and day. Dark, milk, semisweet, bittersweet. It didn't matter. When I couldn't get the real thing, I'd eat baker's ch—eh—chocolate. At work, my friends would Snickers—uh, laugh—at me when I'd make my Mounds—rounds—with a Baby Ruth in one hand and a Butterfinger in the other. I started developing nervous Twix—tics!—when I couldn't get any choco . . . choco . . . that stuff! Then one day, I was at home with candy wrappers all around me and I knew it was time to watch my M&Ms—I mean, *p*s and *q*s. So I quit. Just like that! I just said no. It was a miracle. Now I don't even crave ch—ch—

Opera: Chocolate.

Jim: YES! I no longer need it. Not at all. Un-uh. No way.

Opera: Incredible. You did this on your own? Sheer will power?

Jim: Told myself I didn't want it. And I don't. I don't care if I ever see the stuff again. Told my mind that I did not . . . did not . . . want . . . *(Jim has found an old candy wrapper in his pocket and starts to eat the paper.)* Don't want it! Don't even think about it! *(Opera reaches for the wrapper.)* Touch it and die, Wimpy!

55

Opera:	*(Pulling back.)* Well . . . let's move on to Cheryl Nada. Cheryl, are you here? Cheryl? Cheryl?
Audience member:	*(Forcing Cheryl to stand.)* She's right here! Over here!
Cheryl:	I am not! Am not! No one's calling me—*(Turns and sees Opera and her microphone.)* Oh, hi, Opera. How are you?
Opera:	Just fine, Cheryl. *(Looks at index card.)* Chocolate. Ruler of your life. Filled your head night and day. Yet you beat it. How?
Cheryl:	I never ate chocolate. Who told you that? Un-uh.
Opera:	You told us. On this card. Said you were a major chocoholic.
Cheryl:	Oh . . . *(Laughs.)* well, yes. I had a little problem. *(She pulls out a candy bar and begins to peel the wrapper.)* I used to have trouble with chocolate, but not anymore. I don't even think about chocolate. I never even see chocolate. It's completely gone out of my life.
Opera:	*(Staring at the candy bar.)* Really.
Cheryl:	It's history. *(Holds up the candy bar.)* Hey, want some of this banana?
Opera:	Maybe a little denial here.
Cheryl:	What?! What do you mean by that! Hey!
Opera:	Right. Ah . . . Susan Gunnersma? Are you here?
Susan:	*(Standing and snapping to.)* Present, sir! *(Susan is dressed in fatigues and has vegetables sticking out of every pocket. She eats vegetables as she speaks.)*
Opera:	Susan. Portrait of a cocoa-bean hound. So, what's your story?
Susan:	Met with some chocolate resistance, sir! Assessed the strength of the enemy, sir! Ascertained the need for reinforcement, sir! Went to the Hagelschlag School of Chocolate Warfare in Oak Park, Illinois, sir!
Opera:	How did that help change your destructive eating patterns?
Susan:	Adopted new behavior patterns, sir! Rise at 0500, exercise, eat carrots, oats, tofu, eggs. Then more exercise. Self-help reading period. Lunch: salad, lentil stew and 37-grain bread. Laps, shopping maneuvers. Read *Vegetarian Times* and *Self* magazines. Dinner: soy burger, tofu potatoes, watercress. Lights out 2100 hours. *(Starts doing jumping jacks.)*

dramas

Opera:	With a schedule like that, there's no time for chocolate.
Susan:	Sir, yes, SIR!
Opera:	All right. We've got will power, denial and behavioral modification. Let's talk a minute to Michael Cleanbill.
Michael:	*(Stands with a pound-box of chocolates.)* Here, Opera.
Opera:	Well, aren't you brave? A box of chocolates. Tell us.
Michael:	It was hard. Really hard. I was overweight and feeling bad about myself. I knew I couldn't stop eating chocolate, so I told Jesus I had a problem. I told Him He had more power than I did. Then I started to realize that I ate chocolate because I was angry. I wanted someone, something, to care about me. But this box of chocolates didn't love me. I had to let God love me. Then I could start loving myself. After a while, I just started losing interest in the stuff.
Opera:	That easy?
Michael:	No, not easy at all. But lasting. You want one, Opera?
Opera:	Oh, no, thanks. Well, maybe . . . just one.

She reaches out and takes one, as does Michael. They take a nibble and chew, smiling.

dramas

let your light shine

topics
Modeling Christian behavior; mission work; helping others

key verses
Matthew 5:16; 25:34-40; Ephesians 4:32

cast
Four friends, dressed in pajamas:
> Lindie
>
> Jill
>
> Carrie
>
> Jenny

Lindie's mom, an offstage voice

props
Sleeping bags, cans of soda, popcorn, pillows, a portable radio, a telephone, magazines

scene
A sleepover at Lindie's house. The scene opens with pillow fight. Giggling, all four friends fall down onto their sleeping bags.

Jenny:	*(Flipping through a popular magazine.)* I think [latest TV hunk] is the cutest guy in the world.
Carrie:	Me, too. I joined his fan club and got the coolest picture of him. He even signed it "To Carrie—Love, [latest TV hunk]." That's his real name.
Jenny:	No way! I bet he didn't write "Love."
Carrie:	Yes, he did. I'll show you tomorrow.
Jenny:	Well, I think [another TV hunk] is the cutest. Who do you think is the cutest, Jill?
Jill:	Kevin Costner.
Lindie:	He's cute, but he's so old.

Jenny:	I almost forgot to tell you guys—tomorrow, Jimmy, Paul and Ricky said they're going to play miniature golf at the same place and the same time as we are.
Carrie:	Jill.
Jill:	What?
Carrie:	Oh, I don't know. *(Hesitates.)* Maybe it's because you happen to love Ricky.
Jill:	I said I like him; it's no big deal. Besides, I won't be there tomorrow anyway.
Lindie:	Why not?
Jill:	It's my family's day to be missionaries.
Carrie:	Missionaries?
Jill:	Yes.
Lindie:	What does that mean?
Jenny:	It means people who go to countries with jungles and try to make friends with headhunters. *(Everyone except Jill giggles.)*
Jill:	There are all kinds of missionaries. Some missionaries go to other countries and talk about Jesus with people who have never heard of Him. Others help people who live close to where they live. That's the kind of missionaries we are.
Carrie:	Where do you go?
Jill:	Just around here. Tomorrow we're going to [name of a poor neighborhood].
Jenny:	Oh, [name of a poor neighborhood]—that's where the most dangerous headhunters live.
Jill:	You are so amusing, Jenny.
Lindie:	What are you going to do in [name of poor neighborhood]?
Jill:	We help give food and clothes to the homeless. And we tell them the good news.
Jenny:	The good news is we get to go miniature golfing tomorrow. The bad news is you can't come.
Jill:	The good news that I'm talking about is that Jesus came down to earth and died for our sins, so that when we die we get to live forever with Him in heaven. So, anyway, once a month we help other people and we share about Jesus if they don't already know about Him.

Carrie:	Well, that sounds okay. But I don't see why you have to do it. I mean, you're still a kid.
Jill:	Kids can be missionaries, too, you know. Sometimes when we're giving food and stuff to people, my mom and dad talk to the adults and I talk to the kids.
Jenny:	Well, I think you're crazy to go do that when you could come have fun with us and Jimmy and Paul and Ricky.
Jill:	I can go miniature golfing anytime. Some of the people we help don't even have enough money to have any kind of fun like that.
Mom:	*(From offstage.)* Girls, it's very late. It would be good if you got at least a little sleep before morning.
Lindie:	Okay, Mom.

They all position their sleeping bags. Jenny moves hers over next to Jill.

Jenny:	*(Whispering to Jill.)* That's really nice—what you and your family are doing. I didn't mean to make fun of it. You know me, I just like to be funny.
Jill:	I know. Hey, maybe sometime all of us could go together. It's pretty cool to help other people.
Jenny:	Okay, but no jungles.
Jill:	*(In a teasing tone of voice.)* Go to sleep, will you!

60

behind the mask

topics
Showing kindness to others; loving your neighbor

key verses
Matthew 5:16; 19:19

cast
Bobby, an elementary-school-age boy
Mrs. Clark, Bobby's mom
Dillon, Bobby's energetic classmate

props
A table and chairs, a telephone book, a telephone, a pitcher of juice, a plate of cookies

scene
The kitchen of the Clark home.

Mrs. Clark:	*(Placing juice and cookies on table.)* Hi, honey. How was school today?
Bobby:	Crummy.
Mrs. Clark:	Why?
Bobby:	'Cause Mrs. Larson has this buddy system. We have to be buddies with another kid in the class for a whole week. We have to help each other out with things. *(Sighs.)* I can't wait till next year. Sixth graders don't have to have buddies.
Mrs. Clark:	Yes, I remember you telling me about that. Last week Jason was your buddy. I thought you liked the idea.
Bobby:	I did when I had someone normal as my buddy.
Mrs. Clark:	Who is your buddy this week?
Bobby:	Dillon. And he's not my buddy. He's nobody's buddy. Nobody even likes him.

Mrs. Clark:	And why is that?
Bobby:	He's just weird.
Mrs. Clark:	Honey, none of us are perfect. What do you mean he's weird?
Bobby:	He's totally hyper; he's always running around like crazy. Mrs. Larson has to tell him to sit down about a million times a day and he says dumb stuff.
Mrs. Clark:	Like what?
Bobby:	Stuff that doesn't make sense. Like he's just making up silly stuff in his head and then he says it.
Mrs. Clark:	Maybe when you get to know him a little better, you'll understand why he acts silly.
Bobby:	I don't want to know him any better.
Mrs. Clark:	Well, sometimes we have to do things we really don't want to do. It would be very nice to try to be friends with Dillon, especially if he doesn't have any friends right now. Let's give him a call and see if he'd like to come over and play.
Bobby:	No way.
Mrs. Clark:	Excuse me?
Bobby:	I don't want to! Why can't someone else be his friend?
Mrs. Clark:	School has been in session for two months. If no one has made friends with him by now, I think we should try. I'll look up his phone number right now. What's his last name?
Bobby:	Parker.
Mrs. Clark:	*(Looks at telephone book.)* D. Parker. *(She dials the phone.)* Hello, is this Dillon? *(Pause.)* Hi, I'm Bobby Clark's mom. Can I speak to your mom? *(Pause.)* Oh, she isn't? Are you with a babysitter? *(Pause.)* Oh, well, can I speak to your sister? *(Long pause.)* Hi, this is Mrs. Clark. Your brother Dillon is in my son Bobby's class. We were wondering if Dillon could come over to our home this afternoon. *(Pause.)* Great. Where do you live? *(Pause.)* That's right around the block from us. Our address is 3306 Elm. *(Pause.)* Okay, we'll see him in a few minutes.
Bobby:	Aw, Mom! I was hoping he couldn't come.
Mrs. Clark:	Bobby, you need to be nice to everyone. Remember the lesson you learned in Sunday School last week?
Bobby:	Oh, all right. *(Sighs.)*

dramas

There's a knock on the door. Before anyone can answer it, Dillon runs in.

Dillon:	*(Enthusiastically.)* I'm here!
Mrs. Clark:	Hi, I'm Mrs. Clark. You must be Dillon. It's nice to meet you.
Bobby:	Hi, Dillon. What do you want to do?
Dillon:	Do you have any balloons? We could make water balloons and throw them at people going by your house.
Mrs. Clark:	We don't do that, Dillon. But I'll bet you would like to have some cookies and punch before you go outside and play.
Dillon:	Yeah, I'm starving.

Everyone sits down for snack.

Mrs. Clark:	So, Dillon, how long have you lived here?
Dillon:	Two months. We had to move here.
Mrs. Clark:	Why did you have to move here?
Dillon:	'Cause my mom and dad are getting a divorce. *(Starts fidgeting and bouncing in his chair.)*
Bobby:	Why are your mom and dad getting a divorce?
Mrs. Clark:	That's not a proper question to ask, Bobby. It's a private matter.
Dillon:	It's okay. I don't know anyway. I think it's 'cause I'm so bad.
Mrs. Clark:	I know for sure that isn't true, Dillon. When parents get divorced it's because they don't get along with each other. It is never the fault of their children. Besides, Dillon, you might do some things that are bad or wrong, but that doesn't make you bad.
Dillon:	Can I use your bathroom?
Bobby:	I'll show you. *(Leaves the room, but returns right away.)*
Mrs. Clark:	You know, that might be why Dillon seems so wild. Watching your parents split up is difficult, and sometimes children react in unusual ways. What they are usually doing is trying to cover up the hurt they feel.
Bobby:	Yeah, I guess so. I don't know how I would act if you and Dad got a divorce.

Dillon returns to the kitchen.

Dillon:	Can we go outside now?
Bobby:	Sure! We have a cool tree house. Want to see it?
Dillon:	Yeah.
Mrs. Clark:	*(Dillon exits first. Mom whispers to Bobby.)* I'm proud of you.
Bobby:	Thanks. *(Shrugs.)* He's not so bad, is he? *(Runs out to play.)*

unto the least of these

topics

Reaching out to others; helping those in need

key verses

Matthew 25:34-40; Ephesians 4:32

cast

Kathy Waters

Lisa, Kathy's teenage daughter

John, Kathy's preteen son

Brenda, a receptionist

Mrs. Mills, a patient in a wheelchair

Mr. Fred James, a patient

props

Two tables (for Brenda's and Mr. James's desks), two chairs (for Brenda and Mr. James), two pads of paper and two pencils, a chair (for Mrs. Mills's wheelchair), a blanket (to cover Mrs. Mills's legs), a bookshelf with books (or several books arranged on Mr. James's desk)

scene

A nursing home.

Kathy:	Now remember what I said. Be polite and friendly.
Lisa:	Mom, how come these people live here, anyway?
Kathy:	Well, honey, most of them need to have care from nurses or doctors, but they aren't sick enough to be in a hospital.
Lisa:	Who are we here to see?
Kathy:	We don't know anyone here yet, but we're going to come here once a week and get to know lots of people.

dramas

John:	*(Complaining.)* I don't see why we have to come here. It's going to be boring and I could be playing with my friends.
Kathy:	John, we talked about this before. Many of the people here don't have anyone to visit them. They get very lonely. It will be good for them and good for us, too.
Lisa:	Don't they have any kids of their own?
Kathy:	Some of them do, but sometimes their children live too far away to visit regularly and some of them just don't take the time to come. Okay, let's go! *(Walks up to the reception desk.)*
Brenda:	Hello! Welcome to Hillcrest Nursing Home. How can I help you?
Kathy:	Hi! My name is Kathy Waters and these are my children, Lisa and John. We're from [name of church] and we're here for a general visitation.
Brenda:	How lovely! Just sign here, please. *(Talks while Kathy signs in.)* It's very nice of you to do this, Mrs. Waters. There are a number of folks here who will be thrilled to see some fresh faces. They're especially pleased when kids visit.
Kathy:	We're happy to do it—and please, call me Kathy. Is there anything we should know?
Brenda:	Well, do you plan to visit on a regular basis?
Kathy:	We'd like to come once a week. I was told that this is usually the best time of day to visit.
Brenda:	That's true. I'd like to mention one lady, in particular, who would be so happy to have you stop by. Her name is Mrs. Mills. She doesn't have any family or friends who visit. She doesn't talk much, but I know she would love to have you speak to her. She's in Room 6, but sometimes you'll find her sitting in the hallway in her wheelchair.
Kathy:	Okay, thank you! *(To kids.)* Let's look for Mrs. Mills first.
Lisa:	Maybe that's her, Mom. *(Referring to a lady sitting with a blanket over her legs and her head down.)*
Kathy:	Are you Mrs. Mills?
Mrs. Mills:	*(Looks up, surprised that someone is speaking to her. Nods her head yes and smiles as she looks at the three.)*

66

Kathy:	I'm Kathy, and these are my children, John and Lisa. *(Reaches out and gently touches Mrs. Mills's hand.)*
Mrs. Mills:	*(Holds Kathy's hand and then John's and Lisa's. Looks at each of them with gratitude.)*
Kathy:	It was so nice to meet you, Mrs. Mills. We will be back again to visit you soon.
Mrs. Mills:	*(In a quiet voice.)* Thank you.
John:	*(Whispering as they walk away.)* Why did she thank us, Mom?
Kathy:	For talking to her, John. *(As they approach a door.)* Let's try this room. *(Knocks.)* Hello?
Mr. James:	*(Sitting at desk; looks up.)* Hello! Come in! Come in!
Kathy:	Hi, I'm Kathy and these are my children, John and Lisa.
Mr. James:	It's very nice to meet you. I'm Fred James.
Kathy:	Did we interrupt you, Mr. James?
Mr. James:	Not really. I was just writing a letter to an old friend. But that can wait. Bill's not here right now.
Kathy:	Who's Bill?
Mr. James:	My roommate. You didn't come to see him?
Kathy:	Actually, we're here visiting whoever would like some company!
Mr. James:	*(Smiles broadly.)* I never turn down good company!
Kathy:	*(Glancing at Mr. James's bookshelf.)* It looks like you do a lot of reading.
Mr. James:	Oh, yes, and writing, too. I'm particularly interested in American history. I'm writing some stories my grand-father told me when I was a young boy. He came out west in a covered wagon. He was a miner in Nevada.
John:	*(Suddenly interested.)* Your own granddad lived in the covered wagon days?
Mr. James:	*(Amused.)* He sure did! Are you interested in the Old West, young man?
John:	I sure am! I'm writing a paper about the wagon trains for my history class in school.
Mr. James:	Maybe I could help you with that, John.
John:	You'd do that? Wow. I'd like to share a story with my class that really happened to someone we know. I mean, well, you know, like your granddad. Can we do that, Mom?

67

Kathy:	Sure! Mr. James, if we came back about this same time next week, would that be good for you?
Mr. James:	That would be just fine. I'll be looking forward to it. *(Nods at John.)*
John:	*(As they walk toward the reception area to leave.)* I can't wait to hear about Mr. James's granddad! That is so neat—and Mr. James is such a nice man, Mom.
Kathy:	Yes, honey, he sure is. But keep in mind that even though other folks may not seem quite as interesting as Mr. James, they are just as valuable and deserving of our love and time, okay?
Lisa:	Mom, don't forget I have ballet lessons today.
Kathy:	Oh, I did forget. Thanks for reminding me. We'd better get going—we'll stay longer next time.
Lisa:	Can I say goodbye to Mrs. Mills first?
Kathy:	That's a nice idea, Lisa.
Lisa:	*(Waving at Mrs. Mills in the hallway.)* Bye, Mrs. Mills. See you next week!
Mrs. Mills:	*(Smiles and waves back.)*
Brenda:	*(As the trio approaches the reception desk to say goodbye.)* Thank you so much for coming by today. I haven't seen Mrs. Mills smile like that in a long time.
Kathy:	It was our pleasure.
Kathy, Lisa and John:	*(In unison.)* Bye! See you soon!

dramas

the new kid

topics

Showing kindness; loving your neighbor

key verses

Matthew 25:34-40; Ephesians 4:32

cast

Four friends:

    Brad

    Billy

    Dave

    Trevor

Peter, the new kid at school

props

A table, five chairs, five sack lunches, a bell to ring offstage

scene

Lunchtime at school—four friends are sitting at a table and Peter is sitting on the ground by himself.

Billy:	You guys want to play baseball after school?
Brad:	Yeah, after I do my chores.
Dave:	After I do my homework. My dad says no playing until that's done.
Trevor:	I'll play.

Peter is within listening distance and glances at the four as they converse.

Billy:	*(Whispers and nods toward Peter.)* What's with that kid sitting over there on the ground?
Dave:	He's new; moved here from some other state.
Trevor:	Why's he sitting on the ground?

Brad:	Maybe he's afraid to sit with people he doesn't know.
Billy:	Who cares? Can you believe that math test Miss Parker gave us?
Dave:	I think we had the same test. Man, was it hard! I bet I'll get a crummy grade.
Brad:	Well, I feel sorry for that kid. I moved once and it was really hard to get to know people. We should ask him to play baseball with us.
Dave:	No way. He hardly ever talks in class and he's real smart. I bet he can't play ball at all.
Brad:	Just because someone is smart doesn't mean he can't play ball. Come on, let's ask him.
Dave:	I say no. We don't need another guy.
Billy:	Dave's right, we don't need anyone else.
Trevor:	It's no big deal. If the kid wants to play, we can use one more player.
Brad:	Billy, what about when you asked us if you could play with us? You weren't exactly the hottest player around, but we let you play.
Billy:	Yeah, I guess so.
Brad:	Dave?
Dave:	*(Reluctantly.)* Okay.
Brad:	I'm going to ask him to come eat with us.
Dave:	Oh, man.
Brad:	What if you were sitting there all by yourself? How would you feel?
Billy:	Dave said he hardly talks.
Trevor:	Maybe he's shy.
Brad:	I'll be back. *(Walks over to Peter.)* Hi. My name is Brad. What's yours?
Peter:	Peter.
Brad:	My friends and I wondered if you'd want to eat lunch with us.
Peter:	*(Smiles.)* Okay.
Brad:	Do you play baseball?
Peter:	Yes. I played catcher on the team at my old school in Pennsylvania.
Brad:	*(To group.)* Guys, this is Peter. Peter, this is Trevor, Billy and Dave.
Dave:	You're in my class.

dramas

Peter:	Yes, I know.
Brad:	Peter played catcher at his old school before he moved here.
Trevor:	We could use a good catcher.

Bell rings offstage.

Brad:	There's the bell. We'd better get to class. Peter, we'll meet you right after school by the front door and show you where we play.
Peter:	Okay. Thanks a lot. *(Everyone heads for the door.)*
Dave:	*(As he walks side by side with Peter.)* You're good at math, aren't you?
Peter:	I guess. I get pretty good grades and I like math.
Dave:	It's my worst subject. Maybe you could help me some time.
Peter:	*(Just before exiting.)* Sure.

batter up

topic

Encouraging other Christians

key verses

Proverbs 16:24; Ephesians 4:29; 1 Thessalonians 5:11

cast

Darren, a Little League player

Kyle, a player on Darren's team

Umpire

Other players

prop

a bat

scene

Darren is up to bat, as if the pitches are coming from the audience. He appears to be nervous.

Players: *(Sitting in the front row.)* Hey batter, hey batter, ay batter, ay batter, ay batter . . .

The players begin to call out various insults, such as, "Move in, everybody. He can't hit!" Darren swings.

Umpire: Strike!

Kyle enters from side at Darren's back and stays near the far end of the stage.

Kyle: *(Much louder than other players.)* Hey! You couldn't hit the broad side of a barn.

Darren: *(Whipping around.)* Hey, I thought that you were on my team.

Kyle:	I am. So don't miss next time. *(Darren, miffed, resumes his stance.)* You've got the worst way of standing I've ever seen.
Darren:	Quit talking to me. I've got to concentrate.
Kyle:	Oh, well, as if *that* will make a difference. *(Darren, frustrated, holds up his bat, ready for the pitch.)* Hey, do you think if you hold the bat up like that the ball will hit it?
Darren:	*(Turning to Kyle.)* Come on, give me a break. I'm going to miss the ball for sure if you keep harping at me.

There is a moment of silence while Darren glares in Kyle's direction. As soon as Darren resumes his stance, Kyle starts up again.

Kyle:	Whiff!
Umpire:	Strike!
Darren:	Now, see what you made me do!
Kyle:	Well, don't get all huffy. Temper, temper! *(Darren attempts to ignore Kyle.)* Maybe you should take a class on controlling that anger. And maybe take a batting class at the same time.
Darren:	*(Puts bat down; to pitcher.)* Excuse me a moment. *(To Kyle.)* Can I talk to you, please?
Kyle:	*(Amiable.)* Whatever.
Darren:	If I miss this pitch, we lose the game. Does that mean anything to you?
Kyle:	Sure. It means you're going to lose the game for us. Nice going.
Darren:	*(With forced patience.)* But Kyle, I don't *have* to miss the pitch. It might help if you cheered for me instead of against me.
Kyle:	Nah.
Darren:	You don't mind losing?
Kyle:	Why should I care? It's going to be your fault.
Darren:	It's still your team. And your dad's watching. And the whole neighborhood's watching. What's with you, anyway?
Umpire:	Batter up!

Darren resumes his batting stance. There is a slight pause.

Kyle:	*(Sarcastically.)* Well, if you really want to know, seeing you mess up is more fun than winning *any* day. *(Darren grits his teeth and keeps his position. Pause.)* Whiff!
Darren:	*(Swinging his bat wildly.)* Aaaaaaaugh!
Umpire:	Strike! You're out!

Darren spins to a stop and looks dejectedly at his bat.

| Kyle: | I told you you'd miss. |

the very least

topic
Helping the needy

key verses
Matthew 25:34-46; Luke 14:12-14; Acts 20:35; Hebrews 13:16

cast
Needy Person
Oblivious Christian 1
Oblivious Christian 2
Oblivious Christian 3

props
a chair; a jacket covered with Christian buttons; a muffler; a stocking cap; a Bible; a business suit; an umbrella; a checkbook; a small calculator; a wallet; an offering can that reads, "God Cares"; wallet pictures; cash; sound effects of street sounds (optional); a drum (optional); glasses (optional)

scene
The area is empty, except for a chair. We hear the sounds of a busy street, and then a drum begins to beat at a steady cadence (this will build during the scene). Needy Guy comes in, looking around. He is wearing dirty, baggy clothes and looks disheveled. He sits on the chair, tired, hungry and dejected. He shivers from the cold.

Oblivious Christian 1 enters and falls into a circular march around the chair in rhythm with the drumbeat. He is wearing a jacket with lots of Christian buttons, sayings and symbols pinned to it. He's also wearing a warm muffler and stocking cap. He reads from a huge black Bible and is preaching, mouth going and finger pointing. We watch him for a moment.

The street sounds fade out. Needy Person sees Oblivious Christian 1 and is delighted. He comes up and pulls out his pockets, and then holds a hand out. Oblivious Christian 1 brushes past him roughly. Needy Person spins and falls to the floor. He gets up and goes to Oblivious Christian 1,

dramas

shivering and holding his hand out, asking for the muffler or cap. He gets knocked down again as Oblivious Christian 1 pushes by him.

Oblivious Christian 2 comes in next. He is wearing a business suit and glasses. He has an umbrella under his arm and is balancing a checkbook with a small hand-held calculator. He falls in step with Oblivious Christian 1.

Needy Person smiles and stands. He shows his pockets to Oblivious Christian 2 and shows an empty wallet, watching a moth fly out of it. He holds out a hand. Oblivious Christian 2 brushes past and Needy Person spins and topples to the floor, as before.

Oblivious Christian 3 comes in, dressed officiously and carrying an offering can that reads, "God cares." She falls in step around the circle with the other two. Needy Person stands. He reads the can, smiles and claps and then goes to her, pointing to his pockets and holding out his hand. She knocks into him without noticing, and he tumbles to the floor.

Needy Person stands, upset. He brushes himself off. Suddenly, he feels a hunger pang and stoops over a moment. He shivers. He turns and goes to the three goose-stepping in cadence, faster and faster. He moves between all three, holding out a hand, pointing to his wallet and his pockets. He mimes cradling a baby. He shows pictures. All the while he's dodging them as they pace toward him, oblivious of his presence. He kneels to beg from them, but they bear down on him and he scrambles continually out of the way of one and into the path of another. Finally, he escapes.

Needy Person stands on the chair. He waves for their attention. No go. He jumps up and down. He does a little dance. He pretends like he's hanging himself. No response.

Oblivious Christian 2 drops his umbrella and Needy Person gets down to pick it up. He holds the umbrella up to give it to Oblivious Christian 2. Oblivious Christian 2 sees the umbrella and thinks he's being held up. He steps out of line and waves at the others.

They don't notice. Needy Person points at the umbrella and shakes his head—it's not a mugging.

Oblivious Christian 2 pulls out his wallet and takes out money. He holds it out to Needy Guy, who is still shaking his head no. As they stand there, Oblivious Christian 3 comes by and snatches it, stuffing it into her can. Oblivious Christian 2 looks at Oblivious Christian 3, and then at Needy Person. Oblivious Christian 2 blusters, smacks Needy Person over the head with the wallet and gets back in step.

Needy Person drops the umbrella and rubs his head. He gets into the center of the circle and watches them all go by. He has a hunger pang. He sits down on the ground, arms wrapped around himself. He shivers again.

dramas

76

After a moment, as if falling asleep, he simply falls to his side. Unfortunately, he's now in the path of the others. Oblivious Christian 1 stops dead in his tracks when he reaches Needy Person. The others crash into him.

Oblivious Christian	Hey, what's going on! Who stopped the line? What're you doing? I've got to be somewhere!
Oblivious Christian 1:	I think he's dead.
Oblivious Christian 1 & 2:	Who? What? What are you talking about?

All three stand around Needy Person.

Oblivious Christian 1:	I didn't see him. He was just there. I walked right into him.
Oblivious Christian 2:	Too bad.
Oblivious Christian 3:	The poor man. He looks awful. Like he hasn't eaten for days.
Oblivious Christian 1:	It's freezing out here. I wished I had seen him before.
Oblivious Christian 2:	Hey, there's a rescue mission across town. Besides, Burger King's hiring, right? Come on, I've got to get downtown.

The drumbeat suddenly stops. All three look around.

All:	Who's there? *(They look up.)* YOU?! *(They begin to point at Needy Person.)* Him? WHAT? WELL, HE SHOULD HAVE ASKED US FOR HELP!
Oblivious Christian 1:	I've got a jacket—
Oblivious Christian 3:	*(Shaking can.)* I've got something in here—
Oblivious Christian 2:	Does he take MasterCard?

Silence. They look at Needy Person, and then they look up.

All:	That's not fair, Lord . . .WHY DIDN'T YOU TELL US IT WAS YOU?!

dramas

77

the toolbox

topic
Using God's gifts to serve Him

key verses
Matthew 25:14-30; Romans 12:6-8

cast
Barry, a teenager
Homeless Lady
Grease Monkey, a mechanic
Escaped Convict

props
large, shiny toolbox; a can of tuna; a coin; oily overalls; handcuffs and leg irons; a garbage can; newspapers

scene
Barry runs onstage carrying a large, shiny toolbox.

Barry: *(Calling off.)* Dad! Wait—Dad! Hold up, will you! You forgot your toolbox! *(He tries to catch his breath.)* No, *you* forgot it. *(He stops.)* What do you mean? Wait. Time out. What do I want with this thing? No, no, Dad, it's your toolbox. Aw, is this one of those "You're a man now, you need your own toolbox" routines? Okay, so it's mine now. Fine. So how long are you going to be gone? Dad? *Dad! (No reply. He looks at the toolbox.)* Man, this is great. He couldn't pull the old "you're a man now, you need your own Jaguar" routine. *(He unlatches the toolbox.)* What am I doing? No way. If I touch it, something's going to break. Guaranteed. *(Locks it down.)* Yeah, if something happens to anything before he gets back, I'll just tell him I didn't touch anything. That's my story.

Homeless Lady enters from the opposite side of the stage. Barry picks up the toolbox and moves off. He passes by the Homeless Lady and tries to ignore her.

Homeless Lady:	Hey, hey, pal.
Barry:	Got no change. *(Keeps walking.)*
Homeless Lady:	Wait, wait. *(She digs in her pocket and pulls out a can of tuna.)* Do you have a can opener on you?
Barry:	*(Rolls his eyes; sarcastically.)* Sure. . . in my back pocket.
Homeless Lady:	Where'd you get the toolbox?
Barry:	My father. What do you care?
Homeless Lady:	What have you got in it?
Barry:	I don't know.
Homeless Lady:	You haven't opened it?
Barry:	What's it to you, lady? *(Digs in pocket.)* Look, I think I do have a quarter here.
Homeless Lady:	Maybe there's a can opener in there. You never know, huh? Why don't you open 'er up?
Barry:	Trust me. There's no can opener in there!
Homeless Lady:	Maybe I could use a screwdriver and a hammer or something.
Barry:	*(Shoving a coin at her.)* Here's a quarter. I'm not opening the toolbox, okay!
Homeless Lady:	*(Walks away, mumbling.)* Why do you carry the thing around if you aren't going to use it? Sheesh!
Grease Monkey:	*(Offstage.)* Hey, pal! Hey, buddy!

Barry turns around. He sees Grease Monkey enter in oily overalls and a cap.

Grease Monkey:	Hey, do you think you have a trimensional dual-sided spanner in that kit there?
Barry:	A what?
Grease Monkey:	Mind I take a look? It would really help me out. *(He goes to Barry, who backs away, hugging the toolbox.)*
Barry:	Get out. You're not taking anything from this.
Grease Monkey:	Come on. That's a spiffy kit there. I'm broke down, huh? One look. Okay?
Barry:	Look! I'm not opening the toolbox! My dad gave it to me. It's his, got it? I'm not going to use anything that's in it!

dramas

79

Grease Monkey:	If your dad gave it to you, I'm sure he wouldn't mind—
Barry:	He minds!
Grease Monkey:	*(Throws his hands up in surrender.)* Okay, okay! Don't get all squirrelly.

Grease Monkey goes out. Escaped Convict comes in behind Barry. Barry sighs and turns around. He yells in surprise at seeing the Escaped Convict and almost drops the toolbox. The Escaped Convict has handcuffs and leg irons on.

Escaped Convict:	Nice toolbox, buddy. You think you got a—
Barry:	No!
Escaped Convict:	Maybe a hacksaw or some—
Barry:	Nothing!
Escaped Convict:	*(Gestures at the box.)* What's that there, then?
Barry:	*(Backing away.)* A mistake, that's what it is. Somebody just gave it to me. I didn't know I was going to have to do something with it.
Escaped Convict:	Well, hey, can I have it then?
Barry:	No! It's mine! Now, start walking. *(Escaped Convict doesn't move.)* Officer! Officer! *(Escaped Convict looks around, hunted. He hurries out.)* Unbelievable. *(Looks at the box.)* I don't need this grief. None of it! *(He looks around and sees a garbage can a little ways off. He goes and stuffs the toolbox in and covers it up with newspapers.)* That'll work. When he comes back, I'll go get the stupid toolbox for him. He ought to be grateful, anyway. It will all be in one piece when he gets it. *(Pauses. Wipes his hands.)* Yeah, he should be real happy that I took no chances with it.

Barry taps the garbage can twice and goes out, hands stuffed in his pockets.

choosing a path

topics
Standing up for what is right; testing your faith; being the outcast

key verses
Psalm 25:4; 119:105; Proverbs 4:26-27; 3:6

cast
Five friends:
- Bill
- Carolyn
- James
- Jill
- Mark

props
Bikes and/or skateboards

scene
On a sidewalk.

Bill:	So, what are we going to do?
Carolyn:	Think of something. Just sitting here is totally boring.
James:	We could shoot some hoops.
Jill:	*(Sarcastically.)* Oh, that sounds exciting.
Bill:	Here comes Mark. *(Everyone greets Mark.)*
Carolyn:	Mark, save us. We're falling asleep here. You always have good ideas—please think of something fun we can do.
Mark:	No problem! *(Everyone looks at Mark.)* My brother, Buddy, wants us to help him out.
Bill:	Doing what?
Jill:	Cleaning his car again?
Bill:	We only got a dollar each.

Mark:	This is different. No money, but it's still going to be awesome.
Jill:	All right, let's hear it.
Mark:	Okay, this is the deal. There's this group of kids at Buddy's high school. They messed up Buddy's car yesterday while he was at volleyball practice. They soaped the windows and smeared lipstick on the tires. One of Buddy's friends saw them running away.
James:	I bet Buddy was really mad!
Mark:	Yeah, he was. Buddy's friends know where most of the kids from that other group live. So they're going to get back at them real good and we get to help.
Carolyn:	What are we going to do?
Mark:	Soap their car windows, throw eggs and water balloons at their houses, TP their yards—stuff like that.
Jill:	Yeah!
Bill:	Let's do it!
Carolyn:	Those geeks deserve it.
Mark:	We'll meet here tonight after dark. We all in?

Mark puts his hand out; Bill, Jill and Carolyn each put a hand on top of his. They all look at James.

Bill:	*(To James.)* What's up?
James:	I'm out.
Carolyn:	Why?
James:	I'm just out.
Mark:	Hey, if you're going to flake, you've got to give us a reason.
James:	I'm not flaking. I'm just not doing it, okay?
Jill:	You have to do something with your folks?
James:	No.
Bill:	Then what is it? Are you scared?
James:	Lay off, would you? I'm not scared. I can make up my own mind and I don't want to do any of that stuff.
Carolyn:	Then tell us why.
James:	Because it's wrong.
Mark:	Like you've never done anything wrong.
James:	I didn't say that.
Jill:	You afraid we'll get caught?

82

dramas

James:	I'm not afraid I'll get caught because I'm not doing it.
Bill:	I didn't know you were such a Goody Two-shoes. Oh, I bet it's because you're a "church boy."
James:	Why are you making fun of me? You go to church, too.
Bill:	So? At least I'm not a wimp.
James:	I'm not a wimp either.
Jill:	Come on, James. We do everything together.
Carolyn:	Yeah, you know that.
Mark:	We let you hang out with us because we thought you were our friend.
James:	Just because I won't do this doesn't mean I'm not your friend.
Bill:	You're either part of our group in everything or you're not.
Mark:	That's right.
James:	Look, I'm a Christian. I believe the Bible is God's Word, and it says we're supposed to love people. Throwing eggs and all that stuff isn't right.
Mark:	What those kids did to Buddy isn't in the Bible.
James:	No, but even when people do mean things to you, you're not supposed to do mean things back.
Mark:	So Buddy should just go up to those kids and say, "Thanks for messing up my car. You guys are so cool!" and then give them all a big hug. *(Everyone except James laughs.)*
James:	You know I'm not saying that. *(They all just stare at him.)* Well, I guess I'd better go.
Bill:	I guess so.
Mark:	Yeah.
James:	See you tomorrow.

They don't respond to him but start whispering to one another. James walks slowly away, looking over his shoulder at them a couple of times before exiting.

dramas

83

always tomorrow

topics

Right priorities; respect to family

key verses

Exodus 20:12; Leviticus 25:10

cast

Father

Mother

Cindy, daughter

Jeff, son

props

A calendar, day planner and/or notepads for each family member; Post-it notes for Jeff; a table; four chairs; a telephone

scene

Sitting around a table.

Mother:	Okay, everyone look at your day planner, your calendar or, in your case, Jeff, probably your little Post-it notes. We have to figure out a time we can all go visit Aunt Mary.
Jeff and Cindy:	*(Moaning.)* Do we have to?
Mother:	Yes, we have to.
Cindy:	I forget; whose aunt is she?
Mother:	She's your great-aunt. She's my aunt—your grandmother's sister.
Father:	What day are we looking at?
Mother:	How about this weekend?
Jeff:	*(Looks through a pile of Post-it notes.)* Saturday, I have a football practice and on Sunday our high school group is doing a cleanup project after church.

Cindy:	I have cheerleading practice on Saturday, and Sunday I'm heading up that cleanup project that Jeff is doing.
Father:	That's my monthly golf game with the guys. Sunday, I'm helping Joe's neighbor move.
Mother:	You know, we really need to go see Aunt Mary. It's been almost a year since we've seen her and she doesn't live that far away. How about the following weekend?
Cindy:	I can't.
Father:	I can't.
Jeff:	Me either.
Mother:	*(Looks at her day planner.)* Oh, I can't do that weekend myself.

The phone rings. Mother goes to the phone while the other three talk to one another about their schedules.

Mother:	*(Back at the table.)* We will all be clearing our calendars this Saturday for Aunt Mary.
Cindy:	Oh, Mom, I can't miss cheerleading practice. Besides, Aunt Mary's house always smells funny.
Jeff:	And you have to practically yell for her to hear you.
Mother:	We don't have to worry about any of that. We'll be going to Aunt Mary's funeral. She died this morning.

dramas

what about me?

topics
Right priorities; being forthright

key verses
Psalm 49:3; Proverbs 8:7; Ecclesiastes 3:7

cast
Mom
Carrie, daughter

props
Table and four chairs and a backpack

scene
Mom is sitting at the kitchen table when Carrie comes home from school. She looks up as Carrie enters.

Mom:	Hi, Carrie. How was school?
Carrie:	Fine. Is it okay if I go over to Penny's to work on our science project?
Mom:	In a few minutes. I need to talk to you first.
Carrie:	*(Irritated, drops backpack on floor.)* Great! What do we have to cancel now?
Mom:	What makes you think that's what I'm going to tell you?
Carrie:	That's almost all you ever need to talk to me about.
Mom:	That's not true. But in this case it is. We have to cancel our summer vacation. The doctor said we can't chance it. Brad is making decent progress, but if his blood count dropped while we were gone—well, it just wouldn't be a good idea for us to be so far away.
Carrie:	I can't believe it. Every fun thing we've ever planned to do has to be canceled. It isn't fair.

86

Mom:	You're right. It isn't fair. There are all kinds of things in life that aren't fair. Brad's illness is one of them, but that's what we have to deal with right now.
Carrie:	Right now and all the time—for eight years—ever since Brad was born. Our lives revolve around him.
Mom:	He's your brother and he has cancer.
Carrie:	Oh, tell me something new.
Mom:	Don't speak to me like that.
Carrie:	I'm sick of it. We couldn't go skiing last winter or the year before. Now it's our summer vacation. All we do is wait to take him to the hospital and wait to pick him up.
Mom:	We're lucky he's alive.
Carrie:	Well, I don't feel lucky. Sometimes I wish that he wasn't here.
Mom:	How can you say that?
Carrie:	Because it's true. Don't I count for anything? Almost everything I look forward to has to be canceled. I have friends whose parents are divorced and they spend more time with their kids than you do with me.
Mom:	I'm sorry. I guess I have been assuming a lot. Our focus has been on Brad—but for good reason. Why didn't you tell me you needed more of my time before now?
Carrie:	Because I knew what you thought: Good old Carrie. She's a big girl. She can get along without any attention. So what if all the plans have to be dropped? She won't mind. Well, I do mind. I'm 16 and a half. I won't even be home much longer. What do I have to look back on? Not much!
Mom:	That isn't what I thought—well, not exactly. I suppose I did take for granted that you didn't mind.
Carrie:	Other people get someone to stay with their sick kids so the rest of the family can have a break. Why don't we do that?
Mom:	I don't know. I just can't bring myself to leave him with anyone. What if he died while we were gone?
Carrie:	What if I died? What if any of us died? It could happen any time. You're the one who used to tell us that we're supposed to live one day at a time and enjoy every minute of it. Remember?

dramas

Mom:	I know.
Carrie:	So, what's happened? It's like you're obsessed with Brad and nothing else matters.
Mom:	He's my child. When you have children of your own, you'll understand.
Carrie:	What about me? I'm your child, too. Did you forget that?
Mom:	Of course I didn't forget. I love you every bit as much as I love Brad.
Carrie:	If that's so, why don't you get someone to watch Brad so we can take our vacation?
Mom:	I just can't. Not right now anyway.
Carrie:	I'm going to Penny's.
Mom:	We'll go skiing this winter. I promise.
Carrie:	*(Picks up backpack and walks away.)* Yeah, right!

dramas

a costly pair of shoes

topic
Following wise advice

key verses
Proverbs 12:15; 19:20

cast
Kevin, a teenage track runner
Steve, a fellow runner
Coach, the school track coach

props
two long benches, two track uniforms, sweat suit, tennis shoes, an iPod, shorts, a T-shirt, a whistle

scene
A school locker room containing two long benches. Steve, wearing a track uniform, enters, listening to his iPod. He rocks out to silent music as he walks to a bench and is seated. He snaps his fingers, taps his feet and sways in time to the music. He begins to take off his shoes as Kevin enters, also wearing a track uniform, limping and groaning in evident pain. Kevin drags himself to the other bench and drops heavily onto it.

Kevin:	Man, am I glad this practice is *over*! My feet are killing me. Those last two laps were so painful that I didn't think I was going to make it! It was awful! *(Holds up each foot in turn and looks it over.)* They hurt like *everything*!
Steve:	*(Noticing; lifts up one earphone.)* Feet give out on you again? Sorry, Kevin. Seems like you keep having this problem! They really are sore, huh?

Kevin:	You don't know the half of it. Man, I didn't think I could drag myself to the locker room! *(Gingerly takes off a shoe.)* Ow! I can't stand it!
Steve:	I feel for you, guy. Let me see. *(He looks.)* Hey, that's terrible, Kev! It's all bloody! Maybe you broke a blister or something.
Kevin:	Yeah . . . I must have. Boy, what a mess! And all my toes are raw! They feel paralyzed. I can't bear to touch 'em! Ow!
Steve:	Hey, what're you going to do? The All-City Track Meet is tomorrow. You'll never run with your feet like that. What are you going to tell Coach?
Kevin:	I don't know. I don't know.

Kevin takes off the other shoe as Coach enters and overhears. Coach is wearing shorts and a T-shirt and has a whistle around his neck. He is a military type, commanding respect from the boys.

Kevin:	Ouch! This foot's even worse! It's bleeding and swollen, too! Why did this have to happen to me? *(Long groan. Steve goes back to listening to his iPod.)*
Coach:	What's the trouble, here? *(Sees Kevin's feet.)* Oh, no, Kevin, not again! Look at those feet. Did that just happen today?
Kevin:	*(Reluctantly.)* Not really, sir. It's been coming on all week. I didn't want to tell you, but every practice it's been getting a little worse.

Coach stoops over and picks up Kevin's shoes. He holds them in the air, one in each hand. Steve is curious and lifts one earphone.

Coach:	Well, no wonder! Are you still wearing these shoes?
Kevin:	Well, sir . . . I . . .
Coach:	What size shoe do you wear?
Kevin:	Eleven and a half.
Coach:	And what size are these shoes?
Kevin:	Uh . . . ten.
Coach:	I can't believe it! I told you three weeks ago to get rid of these things. You missed the marathon last month because your feet hurt, remember?

Kevin:	Uh . . . yes . . .
Coach:	And we lost one whole event because you went lame on your lap of the relay at last Friday's meet. True?
Kevin:	Uh, I guess so . . .

Coach is exasperated. He tosses the shoes to the floor. He paces as he lectures, kicking a shoe like a football as he passes it. Steve listens to Coach as he puts on his sweatsuit, keeping the earphones to one ear.

Coach:	Kevin, what is it with you? I explained to you how incredibly foolish it was to keep on wearing those shoes. They're giving you blisters, cramping your toes, and making it impossible for you to hit your stride. Didn't we talk about this and decide that the shoes were wrong for you?
Kevin:	Yeah . . . we sorta did . . . *(Steve moves closer and listens more intently, earphones now pushed back.)*
Coach:	Well, why, in the name of sanity are you still wearing them and suffering such torment?
Kevin:	Aw, Coach. I love these shoes . . . and they cost 80 dollars . . . and look, they have our school colors on the sides, and . . . and everything. Sir.
Coach:	You aren't making any sense, Kevin. You're going to sacrifice your whole career in track. I'll end up having to drop you from the team just because you won't listen to reason.

Kevin retrieves the shoes from where Coach has thrown them. He begins to put the shoes on again, very carefully.

Kevin:	Maybe the shoes *are* ruining my life, but hey, it's *my* life. So I have to make up my own mind. Even if you're right, it doesn't mean I have to do what you're saying.
Steve:	Kev, use your head! Coach is only trying to help you solve your problem. If you would just pay attention . . .
Kevin:	*(Slowly standing, grimacing at his feet.)* I can't, Steve. You don't understand.
Steve:	But he's right! Get rid of those shoes. It's the only sensible thing for you to do!

dramas

Kevin: *(Annoyed.)* I don't care if he's right! I need to find my *own* solution, not anyone else's. I'll come up with something one of these days. So maybe I'll throw them out and maybe I won't . . . but I'll decide for myself what to do! *(Groaning, he limps out.)*

Coach shakes his head sadly as he and Steve watch Kevin leave.

Steve: What a loon! What's the matter with him, anyway? It's like he doesn't even care about the damage he's doing to himself!

Coach: You know, there's a proverb in the Bible that says a fool thinks he needs no advice . . . but a wise man listens to others. *(Coach turns to Steve and points his finger.)* And now, about that iPod you've been wearing to practice all week . . .

Steve: Sir?

real life

topics
Putting up a false front; "walk the talk"; "talk is cheap"

key verses
Exodus 23:1; Psalm 119:104; Proverbs 25:14

cast
Mother

Father

Kathi, teenage daughter

Jeff, teenage or junior-high-age son

Videographer

Video Assistant (nonspeaking role)

Homeless couple (nonspeaking roles)

props
Video camera and several cables (or extension cords)

scene
The living room of the Franklin home.

Kathi:	*(Mother enters the room.)* Mom, you won't believe what Jeff has done this time. You know those girls from school I've been telling you about? I told them that Christian music is as good as any other kind. Well, since Jenny has all my CDs, I borrowed one of Jeff's . . .
Jeff:	. . . without asking.
Kathi:	I went to play [popular Christian music group] for the girls and guess what was in the CD case? Sausage!
Mother:	That sounds like something a two-year-old would do. I thought you quit playing with your food years ago.
Kathi:	It's not food. It's a heavy metal group that plays disgusting noise and *even* more disgusting words.

dramas

93

Jeff:	Oh, look who's talking—Miss Purity herself. Do you know why she's working the community project for church? Only because Billy is going.
Kathi:	His name isn't Billy. It's William.
Jeff:	Oh, really? Willie.
Kathi:	Shut up, you dweeb.
Mother:	Okay, enough. We'll discuss both issues later. Right now *we've* got too much going on.
Father:	*(Enters the room.)* Hi, gang.
Jeff/Kathi:	Hey, Dad.
Mother:	Hi, honey.
Father:	What hit the side of your car?
Mother:	Some trash cans.
Father:	Do you realize what this is going to do to our insurance rates?
Mother:	Probably not much more than what has happened due to your *five* speeding tickets.
Father:	Don't get me started.
Mother:	Don't worry, I won't. We don't have time. Listen everyone. The film crew from *Real Life* will be here any minute to film a typical end-of-work/school day, so we need to rehearse our scenario. Remember, this is supposed to be authentic.
Father:	Okay, here we go. You know the routine. *(Mother and father go back to the door and reenter separately.)*
Mother:	*(With fake sweet voice.)* Hello, children! *(They all hug.)* How was your day?
Kathi:	Fine, Mom. I was just thanking Jeff for letting me borrow one of his uplifting CDs. He's such a kind brother.
Jeff:	And I was just complimenting Kathi on how nice she is to be working on a community project for church.
Mother:	That's lovely, children.
Father:	Hello, family.
Mother:	*(Gives him a big hug. Children do the same.)* How was your day, honey?
Father:	Fine, thank you. Did I notice a dent in your new car?
Mother:	Yes, I'm afraid so.
Father:	Don't you worry your pretty little head about it. Our insurance will take care of it. I'm just glad to see you weren't hurt.

Mother:	Thank you, my love muffin.
Mother:	*(Back to normal voice.)* Okay, that was great. Now, when I was at the shopping center today, I saw a homeless couple with a "We're hungry" sign, so I invited them for dinner tonight.
Father:	What?
Mother:	I thought it would be a nice touch for *Real Life*.
Father:	Do you know anything at all about these people?

There is a knock on the door.

Mother:	Shhh. This must be them now.
Videographer:	*(Holding camera; assistant holding wires and other gear.)* Just wanted to say thank you. You all did great.
Father:	What do you mean, we all did great?
Videographer:	We shot the footage and I'm sure it will be exactly what we were looking for.
Mother:	What exactly did you shoot?
Videographer:	What happened when you all first arrived home. That was the plan.
Mother:	But we didn't even know you were here.
Videographer:	That was all part of the plan. What you weren't aware of was the hidden cameras. But your contract says we have creative license.
Kathi:	Can we do it over?
Videographer:	No rehearsals on this one—it's real life, remember. Bye.
Father:	Oh, great. *(Everyone moans and groans.)* Now that the cameras aren't rolling, is there any way we can get out of having that homeless family over for dinner?
Mother:	Sure. Give them a call on their cellular phone. *(The kids chuckle.)*
Jeff:	I heard homeless people are dangerous.
Mother:	Kathi, get a piece of paper and a pen and write a note. Say: "Dear homeless people: We were suddenly called away so we'll have to take a rain check on that dinner. We'll be in touch. Love, the Franklins." I'll just pin the note to the door and we'll go out for dinner. *(She opens the door and there is the homeless couple. The Franklin family suddenly put on their fake smiles.)*

dramas

first date

topic
Laughter is good medicine

key verse
Proverbs 17:22

cast
The Dowler Family:
  Herb, dad
  Judy, mom
  Connie, teenage daughter
  Ben, 10-year-old son
  Bobby, 5-year-old son
Brad James, Connie's date

props
Several chairs, arranged as living room furniture (e.g., couch and chairs); a newspaper; a small, soft ball

scene
Connie enters living room, dressed for her first date.

Mom:	You look very pretty, honey.
Connie:	*(Smiles.)* Thanks!
Mom:	Herb, doesn't Connie look darling?
Herb:	*(Looks up from the newspaper.)* Hmmm. Isn't that skirt a little short?
Connie:	Dad, I wear skirts this short all the time.
Dad:	Not on dates, you don't.
Connie:	This is my first date.
Mom:	It's fine, Herb,
Connie:	Mom, can Ben and Bobby go into the other room when Brad comes?

Mom:	Whatever for?
Connie:	I don't want anything dumb to happen.
Mom:	Nothing dumb is going to happen. We'd all like to meet Brad.
Connie:	Well, can everyone act normal, please?
Dad:	Of course we'll act normal. Right, everyone? *(No one else responds. Louder.)* Right, everyone? *(The kids nod their heads yes.)*
Connie:	Daddy?
Dad:	What?
Connie:	Be nice to Brad, okay?
Dad:	Sure.

There is a knock on the door.

Connie:	Hi, Brad. Come in. Everyone, this is Brad. My mom, my dad and my two brothers—Ben and Bobby. *(She grabs Brad's arm and tries to hurry out the door.)* Well, we'd better get going.
Brad:	It was nice to meet all of you.
Dad:	Wait a minute. You don't have to run off. Sit down a minute. *(Connie and Brad reluctantly sit on the edge of the "sofa.")* So, Brad, what do you do?
Brad:	I'm a junior in high school, sir.
Dad:	How about work? Do you have a job?
Brad:	Yes. I deliver pizza.
Dad:	Hmmm. Well, I guess there's a future in fast food.
Brad:	I'm not going to do that forever. I'm going to study mechanical engineering in college.
Dad:	That's good. What sports do you play?
Brad:	Baseball.
Dad:	Hmmm. Wrestling was my game. You ought to try it sometime.
Ben:	*(Comes up very close to Brad.)* What's that on your nose?
Connie:	*(Tries to push Ben away.)* Go away, Ben.
Ben:	It's a major zit!
Connie:	Mom, would you shut him up?
Mom:	Come here, Ben. *(She whispers to him.)*
Connie:	Time to go.
Bobby:	*(Throws a ball at Brad.)* Catch!

Brad isn't able to turn around fast enough, and the ball hits him in the back of the head.

Mom:	I'm so sorry, Brad.
Brad:	That's okay. Bye.
Everyone:	*(In unison.)* Bye.
Connie:	*(Peeks her head back in the door.)* Thanks everyone. That went much better than I expected.

to tell the truth

topics
Honesty; stealing; brotherly love

key verses
Exodus 20:15; Proverbs 8:7; 12:19

cast
Robbie, a fifth- or sixth-grade boy
Ted, Robbie's teenage brother
Mom

props
A desk or small table, a chair for desk, several chairs (arranged to resemble living room furniture), a coffee table, a video game case and instruction booklet, a slip of paper that looks like a receipt, an envelope

scene
Ted walks into living room to find Robbie on the couch reading instructions to new video game.

Ted:	Hey, kid, where did you get that game?
Robbie:	From Mom.
Ted:	She just gave it to you?
Robbie:	Yeah.
Ted:	For no reason?
Robbie:	Yep.
Ted:	Well, I'm going to ask her for some money to buy something too.
Robbie:	No, don't, 'cause she said that's all the money that she had.
Ted:	Sounds kind of fishy to me. I think I'll just ask her. *(Starts to walk out.)*
Robbie:	No, please, wait!

Ted:	(Hands on hips.) Oh, so you're fibbing. Where did you get it?
Robbie:	Are you going to tell on me?
Ted:	Maybe.
Robbie:	Then I'm not telling you.
Ted:	Fine. I'll just ask Mom about it.
Robbie:	No, don't. I wanted Mom to buy me one 'cause Jerry has one, but she said no.
Ted:	(Crosses arms.) So how did you get it?
Robbie:	I found some money.
Ted:	Where?
Robbie:	Over here. (Walks over to the desk and picks up an envelope to show Ted.)
Ted:	You're going to be in big trouble.
Robbie:	Don't tell, please.
Ted:	Why shouldn't I? You always tell on me.
Robbie:	I won't anymore.
Ted:	Yeah, right.
Robbie:	I promise.
Ted:	You're lucky I'm in a good mood. Do you still have the receipt for this?
Robbie:	I don't know.
Ted:	Well, look.
Robbie:	(Goes through his pocket and pulls out a crumpled piece of paper.) Here it is. (Hands it to Ted.)
Ted:	Let's take it back.
Robbie:	Why?
Ted:	Why do you think? You stole some money that didn't belong to you.
Mom:	(Enters the room.) What was that I just heard?
Ted:	I was just about to help Robbie out with a little problem he has.
Mom:	And what might that be? (Crosses arms and looks at Robbie.)
Ted:	(Whispers to Robbie.) Spill your guts, kid.
Robbie:	I took some money from this envelope.
Mom:	Why?
Robbie:	To buy this game.
Mom:	I told you that you couldn't have that game right now.

Ted:	He has the receipt. We were going to take it back.
Mom:	Yes, you will. Do you know what that money was for?
Robbie:	No.
Mom:	It was meant for the poor families who can't afford any gifts at Christmas.
Robbie:	*(Looks down.)* I'm really sorry, Mom.
Ted:	I'll take him and we'll return it right now.
Mom:	Be thinking about what kind of punishment you should have for stealing and let me know when you get back, young man.

Mom exits.

Ted:	*(To Robbie.)* I won't mention to her about the fact you lied to me. We'll discuss that later.
Robbie:	Thanks. You're the best brother in the world.
Ted:	Yeah. *(Robbie hugs him.)* Hey, don't slobber on me, okay? *(Pushes Robbie away and they run offstage.)*

dramas

a name

topics

Name-calling; forgiveness

key verses

Proverbs 17:3-4; 21:23; Matthew 18:21-22

cast

Kenny, a young boy

Billy, Kenny's classmate

props

A football and a bell to ring offstage

scene

Bell rings offstage—Kenny and Billy go to recess.

Kenny:	*(Holding football.)* Do you want to play catch?
Billy:	No.
Kenny:	Why not?
Billy:	Because you called me a name.
Kenny:	What?
Billy:	Snail butt.
Kenny:	No, I didn't.
Billy:	Yes, you did! This morning when you were walking behind me.
Kenny:	Oh, yeah. Well that's because you were walking too slow.
Billy:	So what?
Kenny:	This time we don't have to play follow the leader. Come on.
Billy:	No.
Kenny:	Please.
Billy:	You have to say you're sorry, first.

Kenny:	You didn't tell me you were sorry for calling me a name once.
Billy:	What?
Kenny:	You called me Dog Breath.
Billy:	Well, you smelled like dog breath.
Kenny:	So? It wasn't my fault. I'd brushed my teeth.
Billy:	Okay. I'm sorry.
Kenny:	*(Smiling.)* I'm sorry, too.
Billy:	*(Smiling.)* Know what?
Kenny:	What?
Billy:	You're my best friend in the whole world.
Kenny:	I already know that. *(Both exit stage while tossing ball back and forth.)*

dramas

the all-talk gossip party line

topic

Gossip hurts people

key verses

Proverbs 11:12-13; 16:28; James 3:3-12; 4:11

cast

Announcer, a voice from a low-budget hard-sell commercial

Girl, a gossiping teenager

Guy, a gossiping teenager

props

two phones, a microphone, tape player and tape of Announcer's lines (optional)

scene

Guy and Girl each have a phone receiver to his or her ear. They are talking animatedly (not to each other), laughing and listening with intensity. All is performed silently. An Announcer's voice can be heard on tape or from an offstage microphone.

Announcer: Hello, ladies and gentlemen! Are you lonely? Are you bored with your life? Are you tired of those long Saturday afternoons with only reruns of *COPS* and watching your baby sister eat things off the floor to make your existence bearable? Pretty scary, huh? Well, join the thousands—maybe millions—who are filling in all that dead time by talking on the telephone! That's right, it's the all-new All-talk Gossip Party Line! Just call 1-900-4-GOSSIP and you can spend your Saturday afternoons talking with other

104

bored, TV-tired people with nothing better to do than talk about other people! Sure, talk about friends at church, school or even people you barely know. Everybody's fair game on the All-talk Gossip Party Line. Let's listen in on as one user reaps the benefits of the All-talk Gossip Party Line.

Girl: Well, it just wouldn't surprise me about her. If you're asking me, I just wouldn't doubt it, is what I'm saying. You know, with her past and all. *(Pauses.)* Yeah, her past. You didn't know about her past? *(Pauses.)* Yes, her past before she started coming to our church. What? Well, *I'm* certainly not going to dish about it. *(Pauses.)* Ashleigh, are you dim or what? I said I'm not going to tell you about her. You're just going to have to use your imagination. Nope. Uh-uh. I won't say a . . . *(pauses)* warm. No, no, no. My lips are . . . *(pauses)* you're getting warmer. Ashleigh, it would be wrong if I told you—hot! Very hot! All right. But I did *not tell* you that, got it? So, with a past like that you could probably get the big picture about her and you-know-who from youth group. It just wouldn't surprise me, that's all I'm saying. *(Pauses.)* What? Oh, yeah, we really should pray for her, huh? Hey, while we're on the subject, let me fill you in on some other stuff we could pray for her about!

Announcer: *(Laughing.)* Who said gossip can't be spiritual? And remember, don't be afraid to be vague. Letting the other party do some of the work for you is half the fun of the All-talk Gossip Party Line! Let's listen in on this smooth operator.

Guy: It was awesome! I'm telling you, it was a great party. Hey, do you know who I saw there? *(Pauses.)* Mark, from youth group. If you would have been there you would have seen him as well. He was wasted. *(Pauses.)* Yeah. No doubt about it. He asked me not to tell anyone because he was ashamed of himself, so don't tell too many people, okay? Hey, check it out, you-know-who was there. *(Pauses.)* No, older. The one from the college and career group. Yeah, well we talked. *(Pauses.)* What do you mean what *else* happened? Jealousy,

man. How do you know something happened? *(Smiles.)* Yeah, well you're right about that. I am pretty awesome. Well, you just let your imagination run wild—you're going to think what you want anyway.

Announcer: Don't let the facts stop you on the All-talk Gossip Party Line. That's half the fun of it all! Besides, get enough people on your side, and it becomes the truth anyway! So don't be in the dark anymore about what's going on outside your living room. Call the All-talk Gossip Party Line today.

Guy/Girl: *(Together.)* Uh-huh! That's what his second cousin's brother said. I swear!

Announcer: Start taking charge of your life—and everybody else's. Call the All-talk Gossip Party Line today! Ninety cents for the first three minutes, two bits off of someone's reputation for every minute afterward. So call 1-900-4-GOSSIP. That's 1-900-4-G-O-S-S-I-P. Remember, it's not the truth; it's just all talk on the All-talk Gossip Party Line!

ham sandwich

topic

Being careful about what you put in your mind

key verses

Ephesians 5:4-12; Philippians 4:8-9

cast

Jason, a teenager
Mom, Jason's mother

props

a phone, a counter, a table, two chairs, a trashcan, a plate of food covered with garbage (including a banana peel), a fork

scene

Jason is sitting in his room at one side of the stage. Mom is busy working at a kitchen counter on the opposite side. A table and chairs are in the kitchen with a trashcan nearby.

Jason: *(Dials phone.)* Hi, Mrs. Miller, this is Jason. Is Brad there? Thanks. *(Pauses.)* Yo, Brad! How's it going? *(Pauses.)* Aw, not cool, not cool! Yeah. Yeah. Well, I'm sorry, but the deal's off for tonight. *(Pauses.)* I did ask them, and they said no. I can't go. *(Pauses.)* Hey, look, it's not my fault. Can I help it if my parents are pre-historic? They don't want me to see that movie. *(Pauses.)* Because it's rated *R,* for one thing. *(Pauses.)* I know, I know. I told them everybody's going to it, but they just said, *(mocking parent's voice)* "Not every-body. You're not!" It might damage my character or something. I shouldn't see all that *bad* stuff. *(Pauses.)* Hey, you're not telling me anything I don't already know! Listen, that's exactly what I told my mom.

dramas

"Mom," I said, "basically it's a great plot, it's a good clean story . . . that's the main thing. All that language you think is obscene, the violence and sex, that's just the *background*; it's not important. After all," I said, "It's not like when you were a kid. The things I see and hear every day at school are as bad as anything I'd see at this movie." *(Pauses.)* Nah, she didn't buy it, and neither did my dad. You know what they said? I mean besides not wanting me to go? Get this! They actually told me it was a bad example to others for a Christian to be caught up in worldly things. *(Pauses.)* Yeah, you're right. Sometimes being a Christian is too demanding. It's a bummer, all right!

Mom walks to center stage, toward Jason's room, calling.

Mom:	Jason! Lunch is ready! *(Returns to kitchen.)*
Jason:	Yeah, I know what you mean. Hey, I've got to go. Well, you guys have a blast tonight, anyway. See ya!

Jason crosses to the table and sits down. Mom places a plate of "food" in front of him, and then returns to work at the counter. Jason stares down at the plate.

Jason:	Hey! What *is* this, anyway? It looks awful!
Mom:	*(Turning.)* It's a ham sandwich, dear.
Jason:	*(Disgusted.)* A ham sandwich? Where? You mean it's buried under here somewhere? *(He lifts up a banana peel with his fork.)* Look! There's a banana peel on top of it! Yuck! And what's this other junk?
Mom:	Oh, that's garbage, Jason. You don't mind a little garbage, do you? After all, it's basically a good clean sandwich. That's all that matters, right? Forget about the rest, that's just the setting the sandwich is in. Go ahead and eat it.
Jason:	Mom! I can't eat this junk! It makes me sick just to look at it. Even thinking about it makes me sick!
Mom:	Why, you see a lot worse stuff than that every day in the trashcan. I'm surprised at you, having such a fit

over a little garbage! Can't you just scrape it off and eat it anyway?

Jason: *(Indignant.)* There's no way I can clean up this sandwich so that it's decent to eat!

Jason holds up the sandwich, which is dripping and horrible looking. He drops it back onto the plate.

Jason: I'm not going to put this gross, rotten stuff in my mouth!

Mom: I'm glad to hear that, Jason. *(Pauses for emphasis.)* Now I hope you'll be just as careful about what you put into your mind.

Mom removes the plate and takes it to the trashcan where she dumps it. Jason finally catches on, makes a face and groans.

Mom: Gotcha!

Jason: *(Good naturedly.)* Yeah, yeah. You got me.

dramas

SKITS & SKETCHES

skit \'skit\ **1:** a satirical or humorous story or sketch **2:** a brief comic sketch included in a dramatic performance.

sketch \ 'skech \ a slight theatrical piece having a single scene; especially: a comic variety act.

skits & sketches

Skits are something we do for kids to have fun. They are done purely for entertainment. There is no real purpose behind them other than to have a good time with kids and to help build relationships. None of this stuff will make you a great youth worker, but a lot of it can help you on your way. All of these—if done right—work!

1

doctor's office

cast

Patient One, the healthy one

Patient Two, suffering from an allergy

Patient Three, suffering from an itch

Patient Four, having spasms

Patient Five, a pregnant woman

Receptionist

props

Two chairs, sitting side by side; a table and chair (arranged to serve as receptionist's desk); stuffing to make Patient Five look pregnant

scene

The waiting room of a doctor's office. The scene opens with a receptionist sitting at a table facing the audience. There are two other chairs in the waiting room, also facing the audience. Here is how the scene is played out: The first patient, who is only there for a checkup (because he/she is very, very healthy), "catches" all of the diseases of the other patients.

Patient One:	Hello, I am here to see the doctor for a routine checkup. As you can see, I am the epitome of health. *(Flexes his/her muscles some.)*
Receptionist:	Very well. The doctor will be with you in a moment. You may have a seat. *(Patient One sits down.)*
Patient Two:	*(Enters sneezing loudly and uncontrollably.)* I must see the doctor quick! I've developed this allergy and I'm going crazy! Please help!
Receptionist:	There is someone ahead of you, but the doctor will be with you shortly. Please have a seat.

Patient Two sits next to Patient One. Patient One begins to "catch" the illness and starts sneezing, slowly at first but then reacting as badly as Patient Two. Meanwhile, Patient Two's sneezing decreases until it has stopped.

Patient Two:	(*Standing up to leave.*) You can cancel my appointment, my sneezing has stopped! (*Leaves stage.*)
Patient Three:	(*Enters with a terrible itch.*) Please, I've got to see the doctor for this itch. It's driving me crazy!
Receptionist:	Please have a seat and the doctor will be right out.

Patient Three sits next to the sneezing Patient One. After a few seconds, the itching has transferred to Patient One, who is now sneezing and itching uncontrollably. Like Patient Two, Patient Three no longer has an itching problem.

Patient Three:	(*Standing up to leave.*) I feel fine. You can cancel my appointment. (*Leaves stage.*)
Patient Four:	(*Enters with a wild, flagrant, muscle-jerking, arm-flying kick.*) I've got to see the doctor for this ailment. Can I get in soon?
Receptionist:	Yes, please have a seat and the doctor will be with you shortly.

Patient Four sits next to Patient One. Soon the originally healthy Patient One is sneezing, itching and jerking uncontrollably. Soon Patient Four is calm and his jerking has stopped.

| Patient Four: | (*Standing to leave.*) I'm feeling better now. You can cancel my appointment. (*Leaves stage.*) |

Finally, the last patient enters. This patient is a woman who is obviously very, very pregnant.

| Patient Five: | (*Staggers in and sits down heavily.*) |
| Patient One: | (*Notices her, stands, screams and runs out of the waiting room screaming.*) Oh no! Not me! |

2

ruby mae

cast

Buck and Tex, two old cowboys and longtime friends

props

Two bottles, a table and two chairs, two toy six-guns and holsters

scene

A saloon in a dusty desert town. The two friends meet for the first time in many years. Each is holding a bottle.

Buck:	Tex! Tex, is that you?
Tex:	Well, I'll be a cow's hide! Is that you, Buck? I ain't seen you in near ten years! Are you still rattlesnake rasslin'?
Buck:	You know it! Hey, I gots an idea. Why don't we drink a toast a' sars'parilla to our girls!
Tex:	That's a great idea, ol' Buck.

They put their arms around each other, facing the audience, and begin the toast together.

Both:	To my girl . . . Ruby Mae!

They are each stunned that the other said the same name. They look at each other with murder in their eyes, say a couple of "dag nab its" and then begin again.

Both:	To my girl, Ruby Mae . . . who rides sidesaddle.

Again, they look at each other—the anger beginning to grow. A few more cowboy curses are yelled.

Both:	To my girl, Ruby Mae, who rides sidesaddle . . . and who's got her name on the back of her belt!

Both:	(*The anger builds.*) To my girl, Ruby Mae, who rides sidesaddle, who's got her name on the back of her belt . . . and wears a Stetson hat!
Both:	(*More of the same, but a little faster.*) To my girl, Ruby Mae, who rides sidesaddle, who's got her name on the back of her belt, who wears a Stetson hat . . . and wears alligator boots.
Both:	(*Very angry and very quickly.*) To my girl, Ruby Mae, who rides sidesaddle, who's got her name on the back of her belt, who wears a Stetson hat, and alligator boots . . . with silver spurs! (*At this point, they have had enough.*)
Both:	That's it! I challenge you to a duel!

They stand back to back, count off ten paces, turn and shoot six times at each other. Mortally wounded, they both manage to get back to each other—realizing that their cowboy friendship is deeper than oil—put their arms around one another and begin one last toast.

Both:	To my girl, Ruby Mae, who rides side saddle, who's got her name on the back of her belt, who wears a Stetson hat, and alligator boots with silver spurs and who comes from . . .
Buck:	(*In unison with Tex.*) Tucson.
Tex:	(*In unison with Buck.*) Albuquerque.

They look at each other, stunned.

Buck:	Albuquerque?!
Tex:	Tucson?!

They both collapse on the floor and die.

3

the fly

This skit requires pantomime and some exaggerated acting.

cast
Boy One
Boy Two
The buzzing fly, offstage

props
A table and two chairs, some books stacked on the table, a microphone set up offstage, a glass of water on the table

scene
Two boys are supposedly studying in the school library. After a few minutes, the two boys are distracted by a buzzing fly and, after catching the fly, they proceed to play "baseball" with it.

The scene opens with the two boys reading at a table. After a moment, a fly is heard buzzing near the boys' heads. (Have a person offstage with a microphone making a buzzing sound.) The two boys swat at the fly several times. The fly lands on the table and one of the boys catches it with one hand. He shakes his hand to see if he does indeed have the fly. (He hears the buzzing.) They are excited by their conquest as mischievous smiles come across their faces. They begin to pantomime a baseball game.

Boy One signals to the other to move across the room and get into a catcher's stance, as if to catch a pitched ball. He pantomimes that the first pitch will be a fast ball. He winds up and throws the fly fast toward the catcher. (Buzzer offstage makes buzzing sound to coordinate with the fly being thrown fast.) The catcher catches the fly and, because of the great speed of the pitch, gets knocked backward off his feet.

The catcher throws the fly back to the pitcher. (Buzzer offstage makes slow buzz as fly goes back to pitcher.) The pitcher signals that the next pitch is going to be a huge curve. He winds up and throws a curve (a looping buzz). The catcher watches it curve around the room and then finally catches it. He throws it back to the pitcher.

The pitcher signals that the next pitch is going to be a screwball. He winds up and throws the fly and they watch it make several loops before it finally gets to the catcher. The catcher throws it back. This time the pitcher signals that he is going to throw a sky ball pitch. He winds up and throws the fly straight up into the air.

The catcher and pitcher walk around some while looking way up into the air, waiting for the fly to land. It finally lands in a glass of water that is sitting on the table they were studying at. (The buzzer offstage, who has been buzzing this whole time, now makes a gurgling, buzzing sound as the fly eventually drowns.)

The catcher takes the fly out of the water and begins to perform CPR. He does both the heart massage and breathing. (Buzzer making appropriate noises.) After a moment, the fly comes back to life! The catcher picks up the fly in one hand and shakes it like he did at first to confirm that the fly is alive. They hear the buzzing and are so excited they slap a high five, inadvertently killing the fly, which was still in the catcher's hand. They both look dejectedly at the catcher's hand.

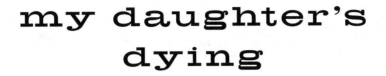

4

my daughter's dying

This is a skit within a skit. In other words, this is a skit of a school play that goes awry. There are five characters who are rehearsing. The "play" is rehearsed a total of four times, with the fourth being the final culmination of all that they practiced during the first three efforts. This skit requires that you have four persons who are absolutely unafraid to "let it all hang out."

cast
Director
Mother
Dying daughter
Doctor
Mortician

props
A director's chair, a broom, a telephone

scene
The scene begins with a director in a director's chair facing a stage where the mother is sweeping the kitchen. The entire first scene is performed in a monotone, lethargic, uninspired and unemotional way.

Director:	Ready, and action!
Daughter:	*(Enters.)* Mother, I think I'm dying. *(She falls next to her mother.)*
Mother:	Oh no, my daughter is dying. I'd better call a doctor. *(She goes to the phone.)* Hello, doctor? *(Pause.)* My daughter is dying. *(Pause.)* Okay, bye.

She hangs up and immediately there is a knock on the door. The mother opens it and it is the doctor.

Mother:	What took you so long?

Skits & sketches

| Doctor: | I had an emergency appendectomy. Where is your daughter? |
| Mother: | She's over there. |

They walk over to the daughter. The doctor bends over and listens to her heart, then lifts her hand and lets it drop.

| Doctor: | Yep, she's dead. I'd better call the morgue. *(He goes to the phone.)* Hello? Morgue? *(Pause.)* This is the doctor. I think we have a dead one. *(Pause.)* Okay, bye. |

He hangs up and immediately there is a knock on the door. He opens it and it is the mortician. They walk over to the body and the mortician examines her briefly.

| Mortician: | Yep, she's dead. |
| Director: | *(Interrupts and yells.)* Stop! |

Everyone stops and turns toward the director, who immediately begins admonishing them.

| Director: | This is an emotional scene! A little girl has just died! Put some life into this thing! Show some emotion! |

The actors all nod their heads in agreement and encourage one another. The director goes back to his chair.

| Director: | Let's try it again, from the top. *(The actors go back to their starting spots and prepare to begin again.)* Ready, action! |

This second scene is exactly the same scene as the first, except that the actors go way overboard in their acting. Every part is screamed out and the emotional content is very, very exaggerated. There is crying and wailing and crawling and screaming. The actors must be extremely demonstrative in their performance. This scene naturally goes much quicker than the first.

| Director: | *(Frustrated, interrupts.)* Stop! Stop! Stop! |

He again admonishes the actors. This time he tells them to lighten up some and not be so melodramatic. Again, they stand up and encourage

one another to do what the director said. They go back to their places and prepare to try again.

Director: From the beginning once again, please. Ready, action!

Again, this third scene is the same scene as the first two, except this time the actors go way overboard in their acting, but this time they are much too lighthearted. They laugh uncontrollably through every line. This scene is the exact opposite of the last—everything is funny! Again, they must be very exaggerated in what they do.

Director: *(Exasperated and pulling at his hair.)* Stop! Stop! Stop! Stop! Stop! *(Once again he admonishes the actors.)* You have all the right ingredients. Now, just put them all together!

They all go back to their places and prepare to try once again.

Director: *(Sighing.)* And ready, action!

This last scene is a combination of the other three.

Daughter: *(Totally lethargic.)* Mother, I think I'm dying.
Mother: *(Screams.)* Oh no! My daughter is dying! I better call a doctor! *(And then continues with her lines.)*

When the doctor comes to the door he is a laughing fool. The three continue their characters until the mortician comes. He, too, is lethargic, but the director stops the action just as he comes in.

Director: *(Interrupts.)* Cut! That's a wrap. Good job.

harry hands and freddy fingers

This skit involves two old pickpockets who run into each other on a city street years and years after their early days as pickpockets. What follows is a funny exchange where these two old veterans sense the ultimate challenge: to pick the other's pocket.

cast
Harry Hands and Freddy Fingers, two old friends and fellow pickpockets

props
All of the following need to be hidden in Harry Hand's clothing (have him wear a big, old coat): a watch, a T-shirt, a large piece of liver (or sausage links). The following items need to be hidden in Freddy Finger's clothing (have him wear a large jacket or coat): a wallet and a pair of men's underwear.

scene
The scene opens with an empty stage. Harry and Freddy walk past each other, inadvertently bump into each other, apologize; then continue walking. After a few feet, they pause and turn toward each other.

Harry: Freddy? Is that you Freddy? Freddy Fingers?
Freddy: Harry Hands? You old goat, you. Is it really you?

They walk toward each other and embrace.

Harry: I haven't seen you since New Orleans. How are things?
Freddy: I'm doing great. Are you still in Tucson, lifting purses?
Harry: No, I've moved up to Chicago. I'm taking Jaguars and Porsches. How about you? Are you still stealing wallets and briefcases in Seattle?
Freddy: Oh, no. I'm in Miami now lifting yachts and large boats. It's a challenge, but it's a good living.

| Harry: | Well, it's been good seeing you. Good luck and I'll see you around. |

They embrace. As they are walking away, Harry suddenly stops and calls out to Freddy.

| Harry: | Hey, Freddy! I'm sorry, but I took your watch. *(He takes a watch out of his coat pocket.)* I didn't really mean to. I guess it's just an old habit. *(Laughs sheepishly.)* Here it is. Will you forgive me? *(Freddy, all the while, is searching for his watch and looking very surprised.)* |
| Freddy: | Oh, it's okay Harry. *(Harry gives the watch back.)* Thanks for giving it back. It's good seeing you. Bye. |

They both start to walk away again, but then Freddy stops and calls out to Harry.

| Freddy: | *(Embarrassed.)* Hey, Harry. I don't know how to tell you this, but, well, I took your wallet. *(Harry is in shock.)* I guess it's true what they say: "You can't teach an old dog new tricks," eh? *(Winks at Harry.)* Please forgive me? |

This happens again, only this time Harry has stolen Freddy's T-shirt. He gives it back and again they part as before. Then it happens again and this time Freddy has stolen Harry's underwear. This would appear to be the end of the scene, but Harry stops again and calls to Freddy.

| Harry: | Fred, I don't know quite how to tell you this. This is really embarrassing, but I've stolen your liver! |

At this point Harry pulls a liver from his coat pocket. The skit ends as Freddy faints.

thar's a bar!

This is an old classic. The line "Thar's a bar!" is actually hillbilly talk for "There's a bear!" This skit has two funny aspects to it. The entire dialogue is hilarious, as is the punch line. The important variable is to make sure that the volunteers all continue to speak in their best hillbilly dialect throughout the skit.

This skit is set up by announcing that it is important to understand how to communicate when you are in the mountains. Ask for five volunteers, then line them up shoulder to shoulder facing the audience. Get in line with the kids, standing first in line on the left end with all of the volunteers on your right. Then tell them that you are going to explain how you would notify others if a bear were around.

Your first line is, "Thar's a bar!" The second person in line asks, "Wharr?" (Where?) You say, "Over thar." They ask, "Over whar?" Then you point straight out with your right hand and say, "Over thar!" The second person repeats everything to the third person in line. This is repeated all the way to the end and the last person then tells you the same thing.

After a moment's pause, you exclaim: "Look, thar's another bar!" This time you cross your left hand over your right. And the whole process is repeated again.

After a moment's pause you exclaim again, "Look! Thar's another bar!" Repeat the process, but this time you get down on your right knee and "point" with your left leg. After everyone has gotten onto their right knee and is now pointing with both arms and one leg, you exclaim once again, "Look! Thar's another bar!" When the first volunteer asks "Whar?" you respond with "Over thar." The volunteer will then ask again "Over whar?" and you say "Over thar," and point with your head right into that person's left shoulder, creating a domino effect and knocking all five volunteers down!

Skits & sketches

pencils

This is another old classic. A man is standing on a street corner trying to sell pencils to earn a little money. He is doing a lousy job when an old friend of his approaches. This friend is a salesperson himself and offers to lend a helping hand. But he remembers that his friend was once knocked in the head by a surfboard and has not only lost some mental capabilities but also has some new twitches and kicks. It is important, though, to overdo this so dramatically that it will be obvious that it is unreal and does not make fun of any particular person or group.

cast
Steve, a person selling pencils
Jack, Steve's old friend
A man reading a newspaper

props
A bunch of pencils; a cup to hold the pencils; a crazy, mismatched outfit for Steve to wear; a nice business outfit for Jack; a newspaper

scene
The scene opens on a busy street corner with the salesperson trying to sell pencils, dressed in a really crazy, mismatched outfit. There is no need for others to be passing by; just announce before the skit begins that the scene is set on a busy downtown street.

Steve: *(Calling out.)* Pencils. Pencils.

Jack, a well-dressed businessperson, comes out of a building and appears to be waiting for a cab. The pencil salesperson approaches him and shoves the can of pencils in his direction, spilling the pencils everywhere. Jack helps pick them up.

Jack: No, thanks. I don't need any pencils today. *(After a moment, he realizes who the pencil salesperson is and happily*

exclaims.) Steve! Is that you? I can't believe it! I haven't seen you in years! How have you been?

Steve: *(Looks at Jack with a blank stare.)*

Jack: Oh, yeah. I forgot, you got hit by that surfboard a few years ago.

All this time the pencil salesperson is oblivious to what is going on. He looks elsewhere, kicks his legs up in a weird way, shakes, twitches, and so on.

Jack: *(Appearing to have some sympathy for him.)* Hey look, I'm also in sales, like you! Maybe I can give you some helpful tips. *(He begins to help.)* First, you have to have a game plan. What are you selling?

Steve: *(Holds up his pencils.)*

Jack: Pencils? Okay. You need to make sure that your product is seen well and heard well. Let me see how you're doing that.

Steve: *(Quietly.)* Pencils.

Jack: Okay, I think I can help. Try saying pencils a little louder—with authority.

Steve: Pencils! *(He says it very loudly and with such spunk that the pencils go flying everywhere.)*

Jack: Good, but a little more under control.

Steve: *(Loudly, but with a little more control.)* Pencils! Pencils!

Jack: *(Pleased.)* Good job! Okay, let's move on to the next step.

Steve: *(Oblivious to his friend, repeats over and over.)* Pencils! Pencils! Pencils!

Jack: *(Trying to calm him down.)* Good. That's good. You're starting to get it. *(Finally gets Steve's attention.)* Now, the second thing most people will want to know is, how much does your product cost. Let's see. You could say "1 for 5 or 5 for 10." Let's practice that. "How much are your pencils?"

Steve: 1 for 5, . . . 6, 7, 8, 9, 10. *(He says this with pride, as if he has given the right answer.)*

Jack: No, no, no. "1 for 5, 5 for 10." Try it again.

Steve: 1 for 5, 5 for 10. 1 for 5, 5 for 10! 1 for . . .

Jack: *(Interrupting.)* Okay, great. Now, people are going to want to know what their options are. So, what color pencils do you have?

skits & sketches

Steve:	*(Holds out his pencils.)*
Jack:	Yellow only? Okay. When someone says, "What color do you have?" you say, "Yellow." Let's practice. "What color do you have?" And you say what?
Steve:	Yellow. *(Then he continues repeating the word "yellow.")*
Jack:	*(Gets his attention again.)* Great! That was perfect. *(Steve continues to ramble.)* Okay, let's get to the fourth point. People are going to want to know what kind of guarantee you have to offer. They'll ask if these pencils will break. You can say something like "Sometimes yes, sometimes no." Try that.
Steve:	Sometimes yes, sometimes no.
Jack:	Perfect! Now, the final point to our strategy is this: no matter how great your product is, some people just aren't going to buy it. So you respond by saying, "If you don't, someone else will!" Let's try that.
Steve:	If you don't, someone else will.
Jack:	*(Enthusiastically.)* That was great. Now you can try this technique on your next potential customer. Hey, here comes one now! Go for it!

The friend steps aside as a person approaches reading a newspaper—his face hidden by the paper.

Steve:	Pencils!

Steve shoves the can into the paper, obviously with too much aggression. The customer lowers the paper and there is a pencil sticking out of his nose—which was planted there prior to coming out. He is visibly upset and angry, but under control.

Customer:	Hey, you jerk! *(Removes pencil.)* You just shoved this pencil into my nose! I just had a nose job! Do you know how much nose jobs cost these days?
Steve:	1 for 5, 5 for 10.
Customer:	*(Annoyed.)* Hey, that's not funny. What do you think I am?
Steve:	Yellow.
Customer:	*(Really annoyed.)* What are you, some kind of smart aleck?

Steve:	Sometimes yes, sometimes no.
Customer:	*(Puts up his fists.)* I oughta bash your head in!
Steve:	If you don't, someone else will!

The skit ends with the customer chasing the pencil salesperson off the stage.

8

lupe, did you see that?

cast

Mother

Lupe, her son

props

Outdoorsy clothes, two pairs of binoculars

scene

A bird refuge. Two nerdy types (a mother and her son) are out in the woods doing some bird watching. Have them dress up in wild, outlandish clothes. They are walking arm in arm, when suddenly the mother speaks.

Mother:	Lupe, did you see that?
Lupe:	No, I missed it. What was it?
Mother:	Oh, Lupe. It was a beautiful yellow-bellied sapsucker! Now keep your eyes open!

Mother and Lupe walk a few steps.

Mother:	Lupe, there! Did you see that?
Lupe:	Oh, rats! I missed it again! What was it?
Mother:	That was awesome! It was a Chinese kitten scratcher! Keep your eyes open, dummy!
Mother:	*(Looking ahead.)* Oh my! Did you see that?
Lupe:	No way, I missed it again! What was it?
Mother:	That was an incredible one-eyed, two-beaked Bahamian boom bird!

They walk a few more steps.

Mother:	Holy mackerel! Did you see that!

skits & sketches

Lupe:	*(Not wanting to miss another bird, he decides to fake it, as if he saw everything.)* Yeah! I saw it!
Mother:	You did see it?
Lupe:	Yeah. I saw it!
Mother:	Are you sure?
Lupe:	Yes, I'm positive!
Mother:	Then why did you step in it?

Lupe looks down and lifts one foot and then the other, making a face.

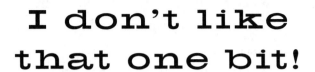

I don't like that one bit!

cast

Alan and Phil, two good friends

props

A day planner, a bench

scene

A bus stop. In this scene, two guys who are good friends happen to run into each other. They are cordial and engage in small talk.

Alan:	Hey, what did you do this last weekend?
Phil:	I'm not sure. Let me look. *(He opens his appointment book to look up what he did.)* Oh, that's right, I had a dinner date.
Alan:	A date! Way to go, man! Who did you go out with?
Phil:	I'm not sure. Let me look. *(Flips through his appointment book.)* Oh yeah, I went out with Angie Patton.
Alan:	*(Disbelieving.)* What? You went out with Angie Patton? That's my girlfriend! I can't believe you! I don't like that one bit! Where did you go?
Phil:	I'm not sure; let me look. *(Refers to his appointment book again.)* Oh yeah, we went to Moose's Restaurant.
Alan:	You took my girlfriend, Angie Patton, to Moose's Restaurant? That's unbelievable. I don't like that one bit! What did you eat?
Phil:	I'm not sure; let me look. *(Turns a page and runs his finger down a list.)* Let's see. She had the surf and turf, salad, baked potato, vegetables, soup, bread, and chocolate mousse dessert. I had a burger.
Alan:	I can't believe you two! I don't like that one bit! What else did you do?

133

Phil:	I'm not sure; let me look. *(Checks book.)* Oh yeah, afterward we went to the beach for a walk.
Alan:	You what? You took my girl to the beach for a walk? I can't believe it! Did you kiss her?!
Phil:	I'm not sure; let me look. Oh yeah, *(snickering)* we kissed!
Alan:	Let me get this straight. Last weekend, you took Angie Patton—MY GIRLFRIEND—to Moose's Restaurant for dinner, then you went to the beach, and then you KISSED her! I can't believe you! *(Yells.)* I don't like that one bit!
Phil:	*(Looking in his appointment book.)* Yeah, neither did I!

10

motorcycle gang

In this fun scene, have four guys on stage lying on their backs side by side with their heads facing the audience. They should have their knees up and their hands up in the air.

Have four people come in looking like rough and tough motorcycle riders (helmets, leather, bandannas, and so forth). They each climb onto a "motorcycle"—sitting on the knees of the guys on the floor—and grasping the "motorcycle handlebars"—the hands of the guys on the floor. The motorcycle riders kick start their bikes (the guys on the ground make the "motor" noise). After all four bikes are started, they take off for a ride.

They need to simultaneously take "turns" together, "pop wheelies," and so on. After about one to two minutes of this, all four bikes run out of gas. The riders try to start their bikes, but to no avail. Then, one biker finally turns and yells, offstage, "Mom! We need another quarter!"

skits & sketches

is it time yet?

In this skit, the more victims—er, "actors"—you have, the better (up to 25 or so). This is one of the corniest skits you'll ever do!

Have a group come onstage and sit in a line of side-by-side chairs facing the audience with their left legs crossed over their right. After a moment, have the first person ask the next person in line "Is it time yet?" That person responds "I'm not sure." Then that person turns to the third person in line and does the same. This continues all the way down. When it gets to the end, the last person looks at his or her watch and says "Not yet." They pass that message all the way back down to the first person.

This whole process is repeated two or three times. Eventually, the last person looks at his or her watch and finally says, "Yes, it's time." This message is passed all the way back down to the first person.

When the last person gets the message, the entire group simultaneously uncrosses their left legs and crosses their right legs over their left.

teenage rumble

cast
Leader One
Leader Two
Eight group members, four to each leader

props
Various silly "weapons," such as paintbrushes, combs, plungers and so forth; bandannas

scene
This funny scene takes place in the backwoods and shows two rival teen groups (not gangs!) meeting for a rumble. You need at least ten people (five per side) for this. Have them dress the part in jeans, leather jackets, bandannas and such. The two groups meet and the leaders do the talking.

Leader One:	So, you guys ready to play by our rules?
Leader Two:	No, I don't think so!
Leader One:	Oh yeah, are you sure you aren't ready to play by our rules?
Leader Two:	No, we're not ready to play by your rules!
Leader One:	Then take this!

The two leaders begin to scuffle and Leader One emerges as the winner with Leader Two left on the ground. He turns to the next person in the other group.

Leader One:	Now, are you guys ready to play by our rules!
Leader Two:	*(Scared.)* Yeah, we're ready to play by your rules.
Leader One:	Good. Let's do it.

At this point, all the people in both groups drop their "weapons" (the paint brushes, plungers, brooms and so forth) and begin to play "Ring Around the Rosy."

monk monotony

cast
Monk One
Monk Two
Sign carrier, a nonspeaking role

props
Two chairs, choir robes, a sign that reads "Ten Years Later"

scene
A monastery. The scene opens with two monks dressed in choir robes sitting in chairs facing the audience. The first monk speaks.

Monk One:	Now that you are a monk and a member of our monastery, are you prepared to take your vow of silence?
Monk Two:	*(Nods his head yes.)*
Monk One:	And you know that you are only allowed to speak two words during the next ten years?
Monk Two:	*(Nods his head yes.)*
Monk One:	Very well. You may go now and begin your ten years of silence.
Monk Two:	*(Leaves the stage.)*

After a moment a person walks through carrying a sign that reads: "Ten Years Later." Monk Two returns and sits next to Monk One.

Monk One:	You have done very well these last ten years by keeping your vow of silence. You may now speak your two words.
Monk Two:	Hard bed.
Monk One:	Very well. Are you now prepared for your next ten years of silence?
Monk Two:	*(Nods his head yes.)*

Monk One:	Very well. You may go now and begin your next ten years of silence.
Monk Two:	*(Leaves the stage.)*

Sign carrier walks through again with the sign. Monk Two returns and sits next to Monk One.

Monk One:	You have done very well these last ten years by keeping your vow of silence. You may now speak your two words.
Monk Two:	Cold food.
Monk One:	Very well. Are you now prepared for your next ten years of silence?
Monk Two:	*(Nods his head yes.)*
Monk One:	Very well. You may go now and begin your next ten years of silence.
Monk Two:	*(Leaves the stage.)*

Sign carrier walks through again with the sign. Monk Two returns and sits next to Monk One.

Monk One:	You have done very well these last ten years by keeping your vow of silence. You may now speak your two words.
Monk Two:	I quit! *(He gets up and walks off the stage.)*
Monk One:	*(To audience.)* Well, I guess I'm not really surprised! He's been complaining ever since he got here!

139

who did I say that to?

cast

Guy

Girl

props

A flower

scene

This skit opens with a girl standing by herself onstage facing the audience. She should be a shy, sweet, friendly girl who is obviously infatuated with the guy who is about to appear. A boy enters carrying a flower and approaches the girl in a shy, coy way.

Guy:	*(Gives girl the flower.)*
Girl:	*(She is all smiles.)*
Guy:	Have I ever told you that I think you are the most beautiful girl in the world?
Girl:	*(Very shy.)* No. *(Sweet and drawn out.)*
Guy:	Have I ever told you that you have the most beautiful eyes in the world?
Girl:	No. *(Sweet and drawn out.)*
Guy:	Have I ever told that I love you and I want to spend the rest of my life with you?
Girl:	No.
Guy:	*(Grabs the flower back.)* Then who did I say that to?

The guy stomps off stage, while the girl stays behind and is brokenhearted.

the really blind date

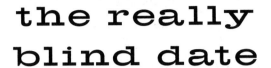

cast

Lynette, a blind girl
Dale, her date
Mother

props

A pair of sunglasses, three chairs set up as a "couch"

scene

The living room of Lynette's home. The scene opens with a girl wearing sunglasses, sitting on a couch. Her mother is behind her sweeping the floor. They are talking (ad lib) about the girl's blind date, who should be there at any minute. They are both very excited about her date. After a moment, there is a knock on the door.

Mother:	I'll get it! (*She walks over to the door and opens it.*) Hello. You must be Dale.
Dale:	Yes, I'm Lynette's date for the evening. Is she in?
Mother:	Yes, she is. Please come in. (*Dale walks in and Lynette's mother excuses herself.*) Goodbye, you kids, I hope you have a fun night.

Mother exits. Dale sits next to Lynette on the couch.

Lynette:	Did Brian tell you about me?
Dale:	No.
Lynette:	Well, I'm blind.
Dale:	(*He begins to make fun of Lynette: he pokes his fingers at her eyes, makes funny faces at her and bends over and sticks his rear end in her face.*) What do you want to do tonight? See a movie? (*He laughs quietly at his "funny" joke.*)

skits & sketches

141

Lynette:	Oh, I don't care. Anything's fine. But there is one more thing you need to know.
Dale:	Oh yeah, what's that? *(Dale continues making a big deal out of poking fun at Lynette's blindness.)*
Lynette:	I'm only blind in one eye.

Dale, of course, is caught red-handed making fun of Lynette. He falls back on the couch, too embarrassed to speak.

16

keep the
worms warm

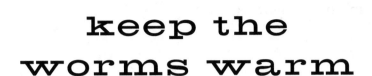

cast
Alec, a yuppie
Walter, a seasoned angler and Alec's next-door neighbor

props
Fishing gear: a hat, pole, tackle box, hip boots; a corncob pipe; night crawlers, or gummy worms

scene
A fishing spot where Alec unexpectedly meets up with Walter.

Alec:	So, you're doing some fishing, eh?
Walter:	*(With a corncob pipe in his mouth and not very interested in any conversation, mumbles without opening his mouth.)* Yes.
Alec:	Having any luck?
Walter:	*(Mumbles without opening his mouth.)* Yes!
Alec:	Wow! What's your secret?
Walter:	*(Mumbling incoherently.)* You've got to keep the worms warm.
Alec:	I'm sorry, I couldn't understand you. What did you say?
Walter:	*(Mumbling incoherently again.)* You've got to keep the worms warm.
Alec:	I'm sorry, I still couldn't understand you. What did you say?
Walter:	*(Takes the pipe out of his mouth and spits out a mouthful of live, crawling night crawlers.)* You've got to keep the worms warm!

Note: This probably sounds too gross, but actually it's not that bad. Here's what you do: Go to a bait store and buy a dozen or so night crawlers. Take them home, take them out of the dirt they came in and wash them off

skits & sketches

with plain water. Then put them in a container and put them in your refrigerator. Just before the skit, take them out and put them into your mouth. They are actually quite clean and not slimy. (For people with weaker stomachs, use gummy worms.)

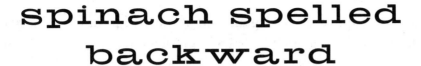

spinach spelled backward

This little skit is ridiculous and makes no sense. It's one of those skits you can do to be crazy, break down walls, and leave the kids dazed and confused. You may want to involve a number of people. At the very least, however, have the listed cast.

cast

Jake

Annette

Sally, the waitress

Bruno, the cook

A few customers

A sign bearer

One volunteer from the audience

props

A large pot of mashed potatoes; some tables and chairs; a sign that says, "What is spinach spelled backward?"

scene

A diner. Jake and Annette walk into the diner, sit down at a table and wait for someone to come and take their order.

Sally:	May I take your order?
Jake:	Yes. We'll have a large pot of mashed potatoes.
Sally:	Is that all?
Jake:	That's it.
Sally:	No beverage? No salad?
Jake:	Nope, just a large pot of mashed potatoes, please.

The waitress disappears offstage and yells to the cook:

Sally:	I need a large order of mashed potatoes.

Bruno:	Anything else? Beverage? Salad?
Sally:	No, just a large pot of mashed potatoes.
Bruno:	What a weird order. Nothing else? Okay, here you go.

The waitress reappears with a giant pot of mashed potatoes. She gives it to Jake. He stands up and sticks his head into the mashed potatoes and gets it all over his face and neck.

Sally:	What are you doing with those mashed potatoes?
Jake:	Mashed potatoes? I thought this was spinach! *(He runs out of the room.)*
Sally:	Oh, spinach. I get it.

With that she sticks her head into the pot and gets the mashed potatoes all over herself. She exits quickly. After a moment of confusion, Annette jumps up.

| Annette: | Oh, now I get it—spinach! *(She sticks her head into the potatoes and exits.)* |

Everyone should be thoroughly confused at this point. Have someone come out with a sign that reads: "What is spinach spelled backward?" Have a kid in the audience jump up and run up onto the stage.

| Volunteer: | Oh! Spinach spelled backward! I get it! *(And he then sticks his head into the mashed potatoes and runs out.)* |

skits & sketches

the italian restaurant

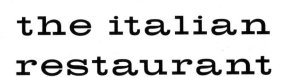

This skit needs to be set up beforehand. Tony, sitting at the table already, is going to exit in only his underwear—use large boxers with shorts underneath. Therefore, he must be in his seat with lower body and legs hidden by the tablecloth when the scene begins.

cast

Luigi, an Italian waiter with a heavy accent
Barry and Jeff, two friends
Tony, a concerned customer

props

Two tables and four chairs, tablecloths for both tables, a large pair of boxer shorts (large enough to fit over a regular pair of shorts), a bowl, a hot dog, a dirty apron for the waiter (must have a mustard stain on it)

scene

At a cheesy, run-down restaurant, the scene opens with Tony sitting at a table waiting for his food. Two other guys—Barry and Jeff—enter the restaurant and have a seat. They are talking about the restaurant and how it has a reputation for things being stolen from customers.

Barry:	I've even heard that people have had their hats, jackets and even their shirts stolen right off their backs.

Luigi enters.

Luigi:	May I take-a your order, please-a?
Barry:	What are your specials?
Luigi:	We have-a soup-a and a hot dog-a.
Barry:	I'll take the soup.
Jeff:	Yeah, that's sounds good. I'll have the soup, too.
Luigi:	Wait a minoot-a! If he has the soup-a, you have to have the hot dog-a.

147

Jeff:	Oh, all right. But put some mustard on it.

Waiter exits.

Tony:	*(To the other customer.)* Did you say they steal things here?
Barry:	That's right. I heard they'll steal the shirt right off your back!
Tony:	Well, I'm keeping a close watch on mine! *(He holds on to his shirt.)* I wish they'd take my order. I've been waiting here since before you guys came in.

The waiter reenters carrying a bowl of soup in one hand and a hot dog without a bun in the other. He drops the hot dog and picks it up and wipes it off on his shirt. He gives them to the two boys.

Jeff:	Waiter, I wanted some mustard on my hot dog. This one's plain.
Luigi:	My mistake-a. *(He takes the hot dog and wipes some mustard from his apron onto it.)* Here you-a go.
Barry:	Waiter, there's a fly in my soup.
Luigi:	Sh. Quiet or everyone will want one. *(He takes the fly out and squeezes it.)* Now you spit all of that out!
Tony:	*(Thoroughly disgusted with the whole scene.)* This is too gross! I'm leaving! *(He gets up to leave and walks out in his underwear!)*

19

echo

This is a little skit that you can use to trick the audience! You announce that there is a certain spot on the stage (or wherever you are up front) that echoes whenever you say something, but you have to find the right spot. You tell them that you are going to try to find that spot and say something that will be echoed.

Search for the special spot, then stand still and yell, "Hotdog!" Listen for the echo. There is none because you are not on the right spot. Move an inch or two over and try again. Yell, "Hotdog!" After three or four seconds, have a person who knows what is going on outside the room echo: "Hotdog!"

That's funny in and of itself, but you continue. "Let me try this," you say to the audience, "Pizza!" Sure enough, after a moment, the echo comes back "Pizza!" Then turn to the audience and say, "Let's try this: Baloney!" There is no echo. You move an inch or two and try again: "Baloney!" Again, no echo.

You mumble something like "I must have moved some. Let me try this one." And with that you yell, "The kids at [fill in your youth group or church name] are really cool." After a moment the echo comes back, "Baloney!"

a day at the movies

This old classic is a skit of two guys who are at a movie theater. There is no dialogue and the funniest part takes place as the skit develops. There are two characters. One must be able to keep a straight face throughout and the other must be a nut!

cast
Moviegoer One
Moviegoer Two

props
Two chairs, set side by side; a large bag with the following items in it: a bag of popcorn, chewing gum, various other items to harass the second guy with, shaving cream; a second large bag with a whipped cream pie in it (set on the floor next to the serious guy's chair)

scene
The skit opens with a man by himself in a movie theater just as the movie begins. Allow him a few seconds by himself to "set the stage." After a moment, have the nutty guy, carrying a large grocery bag, walk in and sit next to him. This guy has brought his own food and snacks for the movie. Remember, the first guy must keep a totally straight face throughout the skit.

The nutty guy begins to liven things up. He's laughing, crying, composing himself, kicking and so on, all while the serious guy keeps his face and body straight and unmoved. After another moment, the nutty guy opens his bag and pulls out some popcorn. He begins to eat it and tries to share it with his neighbor, who never moves and obviously doesn't want any popcorn.

The nutty guy recognizes the opportunity to have fun and puts a piece of popcorn on the serious guy's head. He does not move. So, the nutty guy puts more on the other guy's head, then in his ears, his pockets, wherever he can. He's having a blast!

The nutty guy then pulls some gum out of his bag and starts to chew it. He takes a piece of gum and sticks it on the straight guy. He has fun

with that, sticking it on the nose of the serious guy. Then he pulls some more stuff out of his bag (use different things for this).

Finally, he pulls some shaving cream out and plays little games with the unmoved guy, while squirting shaving cream all over him. This should all take about four or five minutes.

The nutty guy then turns to his bag. As he is doing this, the popcorn-covered, gummed, shaving-creamed guy pulls the surprise ending. He, too, has a bag from which he pulls out a cream pie and pies the other guy in the face! He then gets up and walks out slowly, yet triumphantly. The nutty guy just sits there in shock.

skits & sketches

moo

This skit requires a volunteer to be "planted" in the audience. Three volunteer audience members will be selected and taken out of the room (thus, out of earshot) in order for the rest of the audience to practice "mooing" like a cow. The volunteers will then be brought out one at a time and try to guess the loudest "mooer" in the audience! As the contest gets underway, it cleverly turns into a gag on Volunteer Two—as you will see.

Once the volunteers have been taken out of the room, the audience will need to practice. On the count of three, have the audience moo very loudly in unison. Practice this twice and instruct the audience that each volunteer guesser will get two tries to guess the loudest mooer. Instruct them that there will be no right answers—no winner. The next step will explain why.

This step is crucial. Explain to the audience they are to moo two times for Volunteers One and Two only. Volunteer Three will only be mooed for once, although they will be instructed to moo twice for Volunteer Three during the contest. The gag is that when Volunteer Three has his or her second try, Volunteer Two will be the only person in the audience to moo! Instead of mooing at the count of three this time, have the audience take a deep breath! Don't forget to have the audience practice not mooing a few times!

Now the contest can begin. Bring out Volunteer One (the one plant) and have him/her try to guess the loudest mooing audience member—given two tries. Volunteer One will guess wrong and be told to take a seat with the rest of the audience to participate in the mooing.

Bring out Volunteer Two and do the same thing as with Volunteer One. Now the real fun begins! Once Volunteer Two has guessed wrong and returned to his/her seat in the audience, the audience will be asked to select a person to be the loudest mooer for Volunteer Three to find. Volunteer One will say, "How about him/her?" and point to Volunteer Two.

Now that you've designated Volunteer Two to moo the loudest, bring out Volunteer Three for his/her two tries. Count to three and have everyone moo his or her loudest for Volunteer Three's first guess. Then, follow the same count for the second guess, but this time everyone will take a deep breath, except Volunteer Two, of course, who will unknowingly be mooing solo!

ugliest thing
in the world

This silly, yet funny, skit is also an old classic. Tell the group that you have brought the "ugliest thing in the whole world." You can embellish this a bit, then ask them if they want to see it. Of course they will want to. But tell them this thing is so ugly that only one person at a time is allowed to look at it.

Ask for several volunteers. Have two students "planted" in the audience and choose one of these two. Hopefully, many will have their hands raised so it will appear as if you just chose this first person at random. Bring out the ugliest thing in the world. Have an adult volunteer come out humped over, knees bent, making grotesque noises all while being covered by a large blanket so that no one can see him.

Have the first kid come up to take a tentative look at this monster. Have him/her peer gingerly under the blanket and then immediately have him/her scream and run out of the room. Ask for a second volunteer. Ask the second plant to come up and do the same. Ask for a third volunteer.

This time get any good-natured kid and have him/her come up and look under the blanket. When this person peers under the blanket have the adult volunteer scream and go running out of the room! The joke is that supposedly this third kid is actually so ugly that it scared the "ugliest thing in the world"!

the kiss

cast

Max, a high-school boy, nonspeaking role
Angie, a high-school girl, nonspeaking role
Max's thoughts, an offstage speaking role
Angie's thoughts, an offstage speaking role

props

Two chairs set together to simulate a bench, a bag of M&Ms, offstage microphone for speaking roles, chocolate syrup (to be held in Angie's mouth during skit)

scene

Classmates Max and Angie are sitting on a bench looking coyly at each other. They say nothing and the only action is the guy eating a bag of M&Ms. Offstage, have a microphone set up so that two people (another guy and girl) can verbalize the thoughts of the two people on the stage. The two people on the stage never actually say anything. The only thing the audience hears are the thoughts of the two on stage.

Max:	Boy, Angie is really pretty.
Angie:	Max is such a hunk.
Max:	I sure would like to hold her hand. I wonder if she'll let me.
Angie:	I sure wish he'd hold my hand. *(They move their hands closer together.)* If he'd only stop eating those stupid M&Ms!
Max:	I think I'm going to try and hold her hand. Here goes nothing! *(He moves his hand over and they hold hands.)* Oh, this is so great. Her hands are so soft!
Angie:	His hands are so strong. I wish he'd kiss me, but he keeps eating those stupid M&Ms.
Max:	I wonder if she'll let me kiss her. I think she will. Well, here I go!

They kiss for about 10 seconds. After the kiss, the girl drools chocolate syrup all over her shirt!

hobby hoax

This funny gag can be done to any number of students. First, ask for volunteers. After three or so have volunteered, have a leader take them out of the room.

When the volunteers have left the room, the leader tells the volunteers to think of their favorite hobbies. It could be cheerleading, baseball, football, fishing, writing poetry. Then tell them that when they go back out in front of the audience, the emcee (another leader) is going to ask each of them some questions pertaining to his or her hobby. They should answer these questions honestly. The idea is that the first audience member to guess their hobby correctly wins a prize.

In the meantime, the emcee tells the audience that the volunteers are actually going to answer some questions about their first kiss ever. The result is hilarious.

Suppose the volunteer's favorite hobby is baseball. Here's how the scene might play out:

Leader:	When did you first do this?
First Volunteer:	When I was five.
Leader:	Who did you do this with?
First Volunteer:	My dad and brothers.
Leader:	Did you do this with anyone else?
First Volunteer:	Yes, sometimes with guys down the street.
Leader:	How often did you do this?
First Volunteer:	As much as we could. Usually, every day after school.

And so on. The responses will leave everyone in stitches!

take off what you don't need

This skit is really a gag on the audience. To set this up, you need a large table and a large blanket. Pull one student aside before the meeting begins and clue him or her in to what is happening so he or she can be prepared for it. When you begin this skit, ask for volunteers from the audience. Have two or three come up, along with the person who knows what is going on—the audience does not know that he/she knows.

Have all of the volunteers leave the room and then have them come out one at a time. Have them lie down on the table and put the blanket over them. Ask them to "take off what you don't need." The idea here is that they don't need the blanket that is on them.

Eventually after taking off a shirt or shoes, the person under the blanket will figure out that what they don't need is the blanket. That seems to be funny and that seems to the audience to be the entire skit. But it gets funnier.

Finally, call your last volunteer, who is the informed "volunteer." Have this person do the same routine. But he/she continues to take off what he/she does not need. Finally, he/she appears to have taken off most of his/her clothes. The audience is stunned, thinking that this dummy has just removed all of his/her clothes! But because this person knew what was going on, he/she has clothes on under his/her clothes. The laugh is on the audience.

m&ms commercial

cast
An announcer
A girl

props
A small bag of M&Ms, a small can of chocolate syrup

With a mouthful of chocolate syrup, have the girl come out from behind the curtain and stand in front of the audience, smiling sweetly and holding the bag of M&Ms. Then have someone at a microphone behind the stage say in an announcer's voice: "Tonight's meeting [or concert, or dinner, or play or whatever the event may be] is being brought to you by M&M candies—M&Ms, the milk chocolate that melts in your mouth and not in your hands."

Just as the person says "in your mouth" have the girl spit out the chocolate syrup she has been holding in her mouth, while showing her very clean hands. Make sure it spills out all over her shirt. Lots of it!

duck story

This skit requires audience participation and is quite funny. As the story-teller, instruct the audience that they are to quack from one to three times, according to the amount of fingers held up during the story. Practice a few times, then begin the story, which is told like this:

Once upon a time, there were three brothers, Duck One (hold up one finger), Duck Two (hold up two fingers) and Duck Three (hold up three fingers).

Now, one day, (three fingers) said to his two brothers, "How about if I make dinner tonight?" (One finger) replied, "That would be great, (three fingers)!" And so, (three fingers) made a delicious dinner that evening and they all ate together.

Later that night, (two fingers) began to feel ill so (three fingers) called a doctor, who said "Take two aspirin and call me in the morning." Following the doctor's advice, (three fingers) gave (two fingers) some aspirin and they all went to bed.

The next morning, (two fingers) was dead! (Three fingers) broke the news to his surviving brother by saying, "That doctor must have been a real (one finger)!"

skits & sketches

159

no touchy kung fu

This hilarious skit has no lines to memorize and no punch line. It's actually pretty goofy, except that it ends up being incredibly funny. The skit is a match between two kung-fu fighters who fight in front of the audience in a pretend ring. Here is what you need to do to make it funny.

First, get some good Rocky music (or something appropriate) and have an emcee introduce the two fighters. Next, have a strobe light flashing to add a special effect. Finally, have the two fighters come out wearing only shorts with skin-colored pantyhose over their heads. Have one leg pulled over their heads and the other leg dangling with a tennis ball in it. Have the fighters go through typical kung-fu motions for a few minutes. Then have them begin combat.

The funniest part is that whenever Fighter A lands a punch or a kick, it is he (A) who feels it! If A kicks B in the leg, A is the one that falls to the ground! Remember this is No Touchy Kung Fu. If B pokes A in the eye (like The Three Stooges), B is the one that covers his eyes. Get it? The two fighters continue to do this for a few minutes until either one wins or they both knock the other (actually themselves) out.

the hamburger

cast

Diner (male or female)

Waiter

The cook, must be a guy

props

A table and chair, a tray, a plastic play-food hamburger and bun on a plate, a bottle of ketchup, a glass (or paper cup), an apron, three to four plastic play-food hamburger patties

scene

A restaurant.

Waiter:	May I take your order, sir/miss?
Diner:	Yes, I would like a hamburger and a large lemonade.

After a moment, the waiter returns with a burger on a plate and a drink.

Waiter:	Here you are, sir/miss. I hope you enjoy it.
Diner:	Thank you very much. I'm sure I will.

The diner takes the top bun off of his/her burger and begins to put ketchup on it. Suddenly, he/she stops and disgustedly yells for the waiter.

Diner:	*(Yells.)* Waiter!
Waiter:	*(Running.)* Yes, is there a problem?
Diner:	Yes, there is a hair in my burger. This is totally gross!
Waiter:	I am so sorry, sir/miss. I will bring you another ASAP!

The waiter disappears for a moment and then reappears with another burger.

Waiter:	Here you go, sir/miss. I hope this one is okay for you.

Again, the diner begins to put ketchup on his/her burger only to realize that there is another hair on it.

Diner: *(Yells again.)* Waiter! There is another hair on my burger! I'm about to puke!

Waiter: I am so, so sorry, sir/miss. Let me get you one more. It won't happen again!

The waiter disappears and then reappears once again with another burger. He gives it to the diner. He/she goes through the same routine with yet another hair on his/her burger. This time, he/she is really upset.

Diner: *(Yells once more.)* Waiter!

The waiter comes running again.

Diner: Look at this hair! I can't believe this place! Three burgers and three hairs! I demand to speak to the cook!

Waiter: You wish to speak to the cook?

Diner: Yes, the cook! I demand to speak to the cook right now!

Waiter: As you wish, sir/miss. *(The waiter turns to the kitchen and yells.)* Hey, Harold, there's a customer out here who would like to speak with you.

Cook: *(Comes out where he can be seen for the first time, wearing an apron and no shirt.)* Okay. I'll be right there just as soon as I finish making this last burger! *(And with that he flattens a patty by mashing it under his armpit.)*

skits & sketches

the commercial

cast
Husband
Wife
Announcer, offstage speaking role

props
Offstage microphone for announcer; a table; two chairs; a bag of groceries; a can of dog food; a can of corned-beef hash, equal in size to the dog-food can; a can opener; two spoons

preparation
The label on the dog-food can needs to be removed and placed on the corned beef hash can before performing the skit!

scene
At home in the kitchen

Announcer:	*(From offstage.)* Tonight's get-together is brought to you by Choosy Dog. Choosy Dog, the dog food dogs choose.
Wife:	*(Enters kitchen and begins to empty groceries onto table.)*
Husband:	*(Enters from opposite end of stage.)* Hey, honey. How was shopping?
Wife:	Oh, just fine. Nothing exciting.
Husband:	*(Starts to help empty grocery bag.)* Honey! I can't believe you bought this expensive brand of dog food!
Wife:	But, sweetie, it's Spot's favorite. He loves it!
Husband:	*(Patronizing.)* You can't be serious. Dog food is dog food. Spot's just a dumb dog—he can't possibly know the difference! C'mon, honey, get real.
Wife:	I beg to differ, dear. Spot won't eat any other kind. *(Takes out can opener and opens can.)* Here, take a whiff of this. *(Holds can out for husband to sniff.)* Doesn't that

Skits & Sketches

163

smell great? *(Takes a spoonful and eats it.)* And taste it! It really is the best!

Husband: Hey, let me see that! *(Grabs the can and eats a big spoonful.)* That is good! Honey, you were right. From now on it's only Choosy Dog for Spot.

They put their heads together—cheek to cheek—hold out the can and face the audience as if facing a camera.

31

too tired

cast

Four dead-tired guys
A little old lady
An older man
A gorgeous young woman

props

A pencil

scene

A front porch or steps.

Guy One:	Man, I am dead tired. I can't remember the last time I was this beat!
Guy Two:	You're not kidding. I can hardly move. I haven't been this tired since the day I was born!
Guy Three:	You got that right. I feel like I'm 16 going on 100. I'm whipped.
Guy Four:	You guys think you're tired! I'm more tired than all of you combined! I couldn't be more tired.

The four guys all sit down on the porch, continuing to discuss how tired they are. Just then, an older lady enters the scene.

Little Old Lady:	Boys, my car just got a flat tire. Could I bother you for some help?

The four guys explain they are just way too tired to help and finally say no. The lady leaves, disappointed. After a moment, an older gentleman enters.

Older Man:	*(In pain, holding his chest.)* Friends, I believe I am having a heart attack. Could one of you please take me to the emergency room?

165

The four guys again explain that they are just too tired to help and finally say no. The gentleman, in obvious pain, leaves. After a moment, a gorgeous woman enters the stage and walks in front of the guys. They are all staring with their tongues hanging out. After she crosses in front of them, she accidentally drops her pencil.

Young Woman: Say, fellas, I seem to have dropped my pencil. Could one of you please get it for me?

With that the four guys begin to do battle for the right to hand her the pencil. Only the four guys are doing this in slow motion. (Play some loud action-movie type music and add a strobe light for a great effect.) After about one minute, have Guy One finally win the battle—the other three are passed out on the floor—and get the pencil. Have him hold it up to her as the music and strobe light stops.

Young Woman: (As she takes the pencil.) Thanks!
Guy One: Oh, it's no big deal.

He passes out, like the others.

32

the psychologist appointment

cast

A patient with an intriguing habit
A psychologist

props

A desk or table; two chairs, arranged one on either side of the desk (or table); a couch (or three chairs arranged side by side)

scene

Office of the psychologist. Open the scene with the psychologist at his/her desk. There is a knock on the door.

Psychologist: Come in. Hello, I'm Doctor Hinklestein. How may I help you?

Patient: I'm your 1:00 appointment. Sorry I'm late. I had to take my heartworm pills.

Psychologist: That's okay. What can I help you with today?

Patient: Well, I'm trying to break this—BARK!—nervous habit that I have.

The bark should be loud and surprising. The psychologist should be alarmed yet not shocked—as if he/she has seen this kind of thing before.

Psychologist: Very well. I think I can help you.

Patient: Thanks, doctor. BARK!

Psychologist: How long have you been engaging in this habit?

Patient: Oh, BARK! Ever since I was a teenager. BARK!

Psychologist: Let me ask you this: As a little kid, were you ever frightened by a vicious dog?

Patient: *(Surprised by the question.)* Huh? A vicious dog? I don't—BARK!—get it.

Psychologist:	Well, sometimes these problems can be traced back to an event in a person's childhood.
Patient:	Oh, well this is just a—BARK!—nervous habit.
Psychologist:	Have you tried to break this so-called habit before?
Patient:	Well, yes. I've tried lots of things, like wearing gloves and painting my finger nails with that yucky stuff.
Psychologist:	You tried wearing gloves?
Patient:	Well, sure, you know. I thought if I wore—BARK!—gloves, I might not bite my nails so much.
Psychologist:	Bite your nails? That's your nervous habit?
Patient:	Of course! What did you think I was—BARK!—referring to? That's why I am here!
Psychologist:	You mean, you came to see me because you bite your nails? This is too weird. Look, why don't you come over here and lie down on this couch and we'll talk.
Patient:	Well, I don't think I can. My mom never lets me on the furniture.
Psychologist:	That's okay, I don't mind. Go ahead, boy. Good boy.

Patient hops up on couch like a dog, spins around, sniffs, then sits down.

Patient:	Well, okay. I think one of the reasons I get nervous—BARK!—and bite my nails is because of my mother.
Psychologist:	Your mother?
Patient:	Well, yes. She always made me sleep on a bunch of papers downstairs in the basement. Somehow—get this—she got this crazy idea—you won't believe this—you know, she got it in her mind that I was, are you listening? That I was going around the house—this is crazy—that I was barking like a dog! Can you believe it? BARK! BARK! BARK!
Psychologist:	You think she is imagining this?
Patient:	Sure! She's crazy! She even wrote to one of those doctors who doesn't eat meat—a veterinarian or something like that.
Psychologist:	And what did his return letter say?
Patient:	I don't know. I chased the mailman away and chewed up the letter—BARK!
Psychologist:	This goes a little farther than I anticipated. I'm going to try a game with you. It's called "word association."

	I'll say a word and you say the first word that comes to your mind. Okay?
Patient:	Cat!
Psychologist:	Wait, I haven't started yet.
Patient:	BARK!
Psychologist:	Hold on now. Here we go. Table!
Patient:	Chair.
Psychologist:	Good.
Patient:	Bad.
Psychologist:	No, no. I mean "good," as in "good job."
Patient:	BARK!
Psychologist:	Let's try this again. Ball!
Patient:	Bat.
Psychologist:	Flower.
Patient:	Rose.
Psychologist:	Cat.
Patient:	BARK!
Psychologist:	Dog catcher.
Patient:	*(Angrily.)* BARK! BARK! BARK!
Psychologist:	Very good. I'll tell you what. This is going to require some thinking. I would like you to come back again next week. How does next Thursday evening sound?
Patient:	Um, no good. BARK! Lassie is on that night.
Psychologist:	Okay, how about Tuesday?
Patient:	That's good. No wait! Scoobie Doobie Doo is on that day! How about Monday?
Psychologist:	Monday is good. So I'll see you then.

The psychologist goes to shake his hand as you would a dog who has learned to shake. The patient hesitates, barks loud again, and then attempts to bite the psychologist's hand. The psychologist smacks the patient on the head. The patient growls and then chases the psychologist out of the room.

don't you start anything!

This is one of those great skits where, upon completion, you may hear—hopefully—lots of moans and groans.

cast
Restaurant host or hostess
Casually dressed guest

props
A podium, jumper cables

scene
A highbrow restaurant. The scene opens with the host standing at the podium waiting for customers to enter the restaurant.

Guest:	Good evening. Table for one, please.
Host/Hostess:	I'm sorry, sir. This is a very classy restaurant. You must wear a tie to dine with us.
Guest:	You're kidding! A tie? You've got to be joking!
Host/Hostess:	No, I'm not. I'm sorry, sir. No tie, no dinner.
Guest:	Very well!

With that, the guest stomps out of the room. A moment later, he reappears wearing a "tie" made from jumper cables.

Guest:	May I have a table now?
Host/Hostess:	What is that?
Guest:	It is my tie. May I please have a table?
Host/Hostess:	*(Realizing what the guest is trying to do.)* Okay. I will give you a table. But I am warning you—DON'T YOU START ANYTHING!

the president's farewell speech

Have someone come out and very seriously announce that one of the leaders has been taking a class in American history and would like to give a practice speech for the class. Build this up a little, and just say that this is a very important project for the person and you are asking the students to cooperate with you for just a few minutes. The leader will be very appreciative for their help.

Then thank them and say, "And now, here is _____ (fill in a leader's name) reciting for us President _____'s (fill in any president's name) farewell speech."

Have the leader come out acting very serious and stand in front of the microphone, clear his/her throat, pause for a moment, then say, "Bye!"

Then have the leader become happy and enthusiastic as he/she walks off the stage with a huge smile, continuing to wave and continuing to say, "Bye, so long, see ya! Thanks for coming!"

skits & sketches

what did you have for dinner?

This skit is funny and a little disgusting.

cast
Scott and Brian, two friends

scene
Have two people walk out in front of the audience engaging in small talk. After a few moments, begin this dialogue:

Scott: Hey, Brian, what did you have for dinner tonight?
Brian: You tell me!

And with that, Brian lets out a huge burp. Scott then proceeds to smell the burp, like a wine taster, taking purposeful whiffs of air where the burp was.

Scott: Let me see . . . you had . . . spaghetti with . . . meat sauce. No wait, cheese sauce, not meat . . . a small salad with Thousand Island . . . garlic bread, about six, no, seven pieces . . . two glasses of homogenized milk . . . and a carrot . . . oh wait, carrot cake for dessert.

After a few moments:

Brian: Actually, I just had a burger.
Scott: Oh.

They walk off together continuing the small talk.

stupid cupid

This is a good skit for Valentine's Day.

cast
A guy
A girl
Cupid

props
A bench, or chairs set up as a park bench

scene
The skit opens with a park bench at center stage and a guy and girl sitting on it. Although they are sitting at opposite ends of the bench and are somewhat shy, they are obviously noticing each other.

After a few moments, Cupid appears from out of nowhere and only the guy is able to see him. The guy's eyes light up, and he begins to signal to Cupid that he is very interested in the girl. Cupid signals back that he understands. This takes a few moments and then Cupid pulls out one of his arrows, ready to shoot it into the girl so she will fall in love with the guy.

Cupid then begins to realize how cute the girl is and you can see his mental wrestling match. He finally realizes what he must do and shoots the guy. The guy falls off the bench dead.

Cupid and the girl prance off the stage to live happily ever after.

the garbage skit

cast

A husband

A wife

props

An iron, an ironing board, a shirt to be ironed

scene

At home in the laundry room. The scene opens with a woman ironing clothes by herself. Her husband walks into the room and they begin to talk.

Husband:	Honey, where is yesterday's paper?
Wife:	I wrapped the garbage in it and threw it out.
Husband:	Oh darn, honey, I wanted to see it.
Wife:	I don't know why. There wasn't much to see—just some coffee grounds and some apple peels.

WALK-ONS

walk-on \'wok-on\ a minor part (as in a dramatic production); also: an actor having such a part.

walk-ons

Leader-led, goofy, short skits used for no particular reason other than laughter. Will often cause teens to ask, "What was the point in that?" Remember, walk-ons are just for fun and can be used in a camp, retreat or youth meeting when you want the students to just have a laugh. A walk-on can be a part of a skit night or they are often used as an interruption to announcements or part of a dinner-hour skit. One of the goals of an effective youth ministry is to give your students an opportunity to laugh. It is always fun after a walk-on to look around and see students asking each other "What was that all about?" and sharing a fun moment.

dr. batos

At the appropriate time, crank on the theme song from 2001: A Space Odyssey (also available as "Thus Spoke Zarathustra" by Richard Strauss) and have "Dr. Batos" walk onstage. This song is readily available from any music store or can be downloaded from a site such as iTunes. Dr. Batos should be dressed in a funky outfit. You might design a costume, using a large white jumpsuit (available at paint supply stores) with a white ski-type mask, white gloves, and a zany pair of sunglasses. The crazier you can make this outfit, the better.

Dr. Batos interrupts the meeting. As everyone in the group gets quiet, the leader speaks.

Leader:	What in the world are you doing?! We're trying to have our meeting here. What is going on? Who are you?
Dr. Batos:	I am Dr. Batos. I can do AMAZING things!
Leader:	Dr. Batos? This is crazy! I've never heard of you! *(Addressing the group.)* Do you want to see Dr. Batos do amazing things? *(They will, of course, yell yes!)* Okay, go ahead and show us, but hurry, we have to finish our meeting. What amazing things are you going to do?
Dr. Batos:	I am going to levitate!
Leader:	Levitate? You can't levitate. That's impossible.
Dr. Batos:	Yes I can. I want everyone to count to three, and when you are done I will levitate. Ready . . . one . . . two . . . three . . .

When the audience says three, Dr. Batos jumps into the air and lands. This is his way of levitating. He raises his hands triumphantly as if he has just done an amazing thing. After everyone gets quiet, Dr. Batos speaks.

Dr. Batos:	I did it!
Leader:	You didn't do it. You didn't levitate. That was crazy! You didn't do it!
Dr. Batos:	I didn't?

Leader:	No, you didn't. In fact, you can't levitate!
Dr. Batos:	I can't?
Leader:	No! And you'll never levitate.
Dr. Batos:	I won't?
Leader:	No, now get out of here and stop wasting our time.

Dr. Batos puts his head down and exits. Usually, the kids will feel very sorry for him.

Do this for four or five weeks or different times in one meeting. Each time Dr. Batos does something that is impossible, but he thinks he accomplishes it. For example, Dr. Batos could "knock down a wall with his bare hands," like knocking on someone's front door. He could "make the audience disappear" by having everyone close their eyes for three seconds. Or he could do a backflip by rolling over in a backwards somersault on the floor.

To end this walk-on, have Dr. Batos finally do something possible.

walk-ons

2

taking my case
to court

In the middle of your meeting, have a leader walk through in a nice suit carrying a briefcase. He or she is obviously interrupting things. Finally, stop him or her and ask, "What in the world are you doing?"

He or she answers, "Oh, just taking my case to court."

In 10 minutes, repeat the interruption, but this time the leader with the briefcase walks through carrying a ladder. When you ask him or her what he/she is doing, he/she answers, "I'm taking my case to a higher court."

walk-ons

three against a thousand

Three leaders walk through the meeting looking like they were just in a riot. Have their heads bandaged, arms wrapped, limping and so forth. After a few moments, stop them and ask, "What in the world are you doing? What happened to all of you?"

One of the three leaders answers, "You wouldn't believe it. We were just in the fight of our lives. Three against a thousand. It was amazing. We're lucky to be alive." They continue to walk for a moment, and then the leader turns and says, "Those three guys were incredible!"

4

two coats

Have a leader walk through your meeting wearing two heavy winter coats and carrying a bucket of paint.

Meeting leader:	Hey, what are you doing?
Second leader:	I'm going to paint my house.
Meeting leader:	But why are you wearing two winter coats? It's hot in here.
Second leader:	I know, but the instructions on the paint can said to put on two coats.

walk-ons

183

INDEXES

index \in-deks\ a list (as of bibliographical information or citations to a body of literature) arranged usually in alphabetical order of some specified datum (as author, subject, or keyword).

scripture index

subject index

contributors

Lawrence G. Enscoe
Andrea J. Enscoe
Robin Jones Gunn
Barbara D. Larsen
Joel Lusz
Marco Palmer
Judith L. Roth
Jim Suth
Lisa Suth
Christine Stanfield

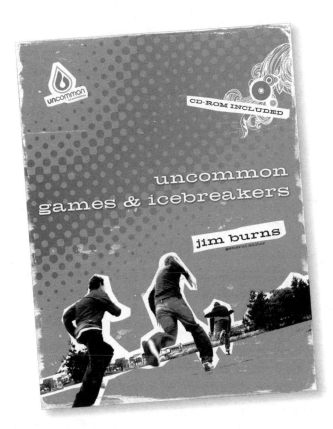
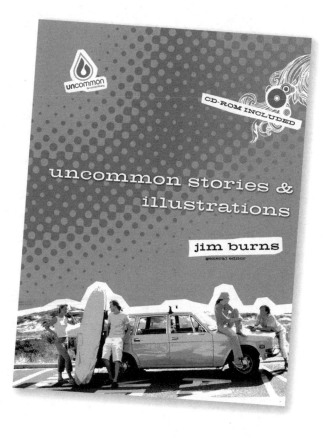